Missionary Priest

A Spiritual Memoir

Thomas Ryan, CSP

I0877003

Paulist Press
New York / Mahwah, NJ

Cover image by The Missionary Society of St. Paul the Apostle
Cover design by Sharyn Banks
Book design by Lynn Else

Copyright © 2024 by Rev. Thomas Ryan

All rights reserved. No part of this publication may be reproduced, stored in a retrieval system, or transmitted in any form or by any means, electronic, mechanical, photocopying, recording, scanning, or otherwise, without either the prior written permission of the Publisher, or authorization through payment of the appropriate per-copy fee to the Copyright Clearance Center, Inc., www.copyright.com. Requests to the Publisher for permission should be addressed to the Permissions Department, Paulist Press, permissions@paulistpress.com.

Library of Congress Cataloging-in-Publication Data
Names: Ryan, Thomas, 1946– author.
Title: Missionary priest : a spiritual memoir / Thomas Ryan.
Description: New York ; Mahwah, NJ : Paulist Press, [2024] | Includes bibliographical references. | Summary: "The autobiography of Paulist Father Thomas Ryan, starting with his upbringing in Minnesota, through his time as a Salesian and ultimately as a member of the Missionary Society of St. Paul the Apostle, covering his years of education and ministry"—Provided by publisher.
Identifiers: LCCN 2023021885 (print) | LCCN 2023021886 (ebook) | ISBN 9780809156818 (paperback) | ISBN 9780809188475 (ebook)
Subjects: LCSH: Ryan, Thomas, 1946– | Catholic Church—Clergy—Biography. | Priests—United States—Biography. | Priests—Canada—Biography.
Classification: LCC BX4668.3.R93 A3 2024 (print) | LCC BX4668.3.R93 (ebook) | DDC 282.092—dc23/eng/20231027
LC record available at https://lccn.loc.gov/2023021885
LC ebook record available at https://lccn.loc.gov/2023021886

ISBN 978-0-8091-5681-8 (paperback)
ISBN 978-0-8091-8847-5 (e-book)

Published by Paulist Press
997 Macarthur Boulevard
Mahwah, New Jersey 07430
www.paulistpress.com

Printed and bound in the
United States of America

CONTENTS

INTRODUCTION

I grew up in the small town of Bird Island in southern Minnesota. There were about 1,200 inhabitants, and our family home was right next to the home of my dad's father and mother, with dad's sister and her family living just a few blocks away. Dad and Grandpa ran Ryan Grain and Feed Elevator for the surrounding rural community. I had just finished my sixth year in St. Mary's grade school a block away from our home when, upon my grandpa's retirement, dad and grandpa decided to sell the elevator. Dad was going to stay engaged with the grain and feed business, but in a new manner: serving as a district sales manager for Ralston Purina Grain and Feed Company. That occasioned a move for our family from Bird Island to the city of Mankato, Minnesota, where I then finished grade school and went to Loyola High School. Sports became an increasingly significant activity and enlivened my life in every season of the year. In my senior year I was an all-state running back and captained our football team to the Minnesota state championship. In track and field, I won the low hurdles in the state meet. Basketball and baseball filled in the other seasons.

I did not view sports, however, as my lifetime career. Rather, I felt called to religious life and joined the Salesians of Don Bosco in Newton, New Jersey, doing my college studies at Don Bosco College there. Once I had completed my studies, I was sent to teach at St. John Bosco High School in Los Angeles. The classes assigned to me were English Literature and California Civics, as well as coaching in football and track. After about a year and a half, however, while enjoying the interactions with the high schoolers, I was not finding fulfillment in teaching literature and civics. I was feeling within myself a desire for a more faith-based content and ministry. Along the way I met some members of another religious community, the Paulist Fathers, whose ministerial opportunities, while varied, struck me as more "on target" for what I was yearning for. I decided to step back from my assignment at the Los Angeles high school and to spend a year at St. Paul's College in Washington, DC, to get to know the Paulists better.

In that transition year, I felt "outward bound" and decided to participate in a program in my home state of Minnesota by that very name: Outward Bound. It's a program in which one spends a month or so in the northern Minnesota Boundary Waters Canoe Area (BWCA) lake country wilderness with a small group of about a half dozen people. If you're in a phase of your life in which you're trying to show people that you *can* do something, even though you're not sure about that within yourself, Outward Bound can be a timely experience.

It involved rock climbing and cliff rappelling at Lake Superior. Rappelling was fun, but to say the least, it's a new sensation to be going into space backward, in contact with nothing but the rope in your hands. In the transitory life situation I was in, it was a test of my ability to trust the people and things that were holding my life in their hands not only through these various activities but through the broader scheme of my life as well. The rappelling cliff was about 150 feet high, straight down most of the way, and you're just hanging by your rope and belt attachment as you feed the rope through your hands to let yourself down.

I found rock climbing more difficult, requiring about ten times more concentration and effort than rappelling. The techniques really make a difference. An untrained person would not dream of climbing some of the rock and boulder walls that we climbed. You learn to use the smallest niches for fingerholds, the most insignificant jutting for the toe rests, and the tiniest cracks in a rock become lifesavers.

In one of the afternoon outings, we went up the Kawis Liwi River and practiced ferrying across the rapids, which the river turns into and out of, giving us the opportunity for shooting the white-water rapids. We stayed at it until each of us had mastered the strokes that the paddlers in both the bow and stern must use in white water.

I experienced a feeling of fear heading into the rapids at the bow of the canoe—a fear more distinct than any I had experienced in rock climbing and cliff rappelling. Perhaps because the latter two afford a feeling of greater control in as much as you can proceed at your own rate. In the rapids you don't have time to think when you see the rocks moving at you through churning waters. You have to react instinctively or you can total the canoe and end up in "the drink."

My BWCA experience helped me come closer to realizing a wish expressed by Henry David Thoreau when he explained why he went into the woods to live. "When I come to the end of my life, I do not want to look back and say that I have not tasted of the heights and depths that life has to offer."

I'm sure that "tasting the heights and depths" is a lifelong process requiring an attitude of continual openness and risk-taking, but at this juncture of my life, I felt I said yes to the fullest opportunities at hand.

Following the Outward Bound summer experience, I joined the Paulist Fathers seminary community in Washington, DC, and entered into three years of graduate studies in theology at the Washington Theological Union.

Part One

VARIOUS MINISTRIES

Chapter 1

CAMPUS MINISTRY

After ordination to the deaconate in 1974, I was assigned to the St. Thomas More Newman Center at Ohio State University in Columbus, Ohio, and after ordination to the priesthood a year later was reassigned there. The Newman Center is a large facility just across the street from the campus with staff offices and meeting rooms, a very large worship hall for weekend liturgies, and a smaller chapel for daily liturgy, with the Paulist residence just a few houses away.

At the time, there were about 56,000 students in daily movement across the huge campus. Our weekend worship was a highlight of each week with our wonderful liturgical music forty-piece orchestral group leading the singing in the large worship hall filled with students and local young couples and their kids. In the course of the week, my days would be filled by students coming to share and seek counseling regarding their faith questions and relational struggles. Even when the students were gone on vacation, there was a steady flow of other people who would call in and come over to seek input on some of the issues they were facing.

Their sharing heightened my awareness for my own need for solid, mature, adult friends, people whom I could be with in a non-problem-solving way, people who didn't look to me in a counselor-counselee kind of way. Friends with whom I could just "share life," as in the day when my friend John and I spent a relaxing afternoon sitting in front of the fireplace in his home talking about cross-country skiing. Then we took a walk through Darby Creek Park, one I'd never been to before. I felt very good and relaxed when I left. It was an enriching sharing.

We all need a few people with whom we can come together the majority of the time around non-problem-centered concerns. I was certainly open to listening to the problems and struggles of my friends, but if in most cases we came together because they had a problem, then there were two messages for me: (1) People, even my "friends," don't feel free to call upon my time unless they have a "problem." (2) If I stay in the minister/counselor role all the time, can I be in relationship with people in a way in which I am not cast as "helper" but simply "sharer"? I wanted to start taking more time just to drop in on people and be with them, with no need for there to be a "problem" occasioning our get-together.

In my college years I began working with junior high schoolers, moved to senior high students, and then in my first Paulist assignment progressed to serving undergrads, graduate students, and married couples. I tended to be a popular figure with the college students because I was young, healthy, athletic, and loved the outdoors.

The lifestyle of singleness allowed me to share in the lives, joys, and struggles of so many people. A couple with their new baby boy; a conversation with family over supper; with a single person over her loneliness. When I stopped to reflect on it, there were many signs of friendship from people who came in and out of each day: the rose from Linda; the piece of cake from Kathy; the cheesecake from Mark and Rosie. I felt like there was so much going for me, so much gift, that it just made me want to be really generous by way of a grateful response. My prayer was often along the lines of "Lord, you have poured out so much upon me. Help me to use my time and talents in a way befitting a grateful heart."

Our life in the Paulist community at the Ohio State University Newman Center was an anchor for all these relationships. We were getting along well, and it gave each of the five of us a rootedness and opportunity for meaningful sharing of our priestly experiences, the people we were meeting, how we were learning to relate comfortably with all kinds of different people—sharing that left me feeling very rich and blessed. As one of my confreres, George Fitzgerald, who had also been my seminary director, said, "Priests are generally able to talk intelligently with people about a whole range of subjects. They are able to relate easily and smoothly with all kinds of people because of their ministerial experience."

There has to be in the life of a priest, however, a relationship at the deepest inner level, an experience of the presence of an Other that is real, personal, and compelling. When I was ordained, I told the Lord "I am committing myself to having you as that Presence, my Lord. I need you. I really need you. Without you, I can't do it. This is why I must take my commitment to prayer with utmost seriousness. To have a spiritual director, and to deeply commit myself to becoming a man of the Spirit. Without this, Lord, I will not come to know you more intimately, and if that does not happen, I will likely leave serving you in the priesthood. So, Lord, draw me. Compel me. Reveal yourself to me. Draw my heart and don't let me stray. I want to be faithful, Lord."

I desired to build my life around the Lord in an explicit way. I wanted to use my time, energy, and talents to share with people in the areas that are a passion for me, that compel me. To spend my time dealing with people around the really big questions in life. I wanted to live at a more profound level and saw this vocation of ministry keeping me right there, growing through the ministerial engagements and becoming a deeper person. It was a happy sense of vocation and avocation.

The opportunity for relationships in the ministry abounded, with students, couples, and single men and women. One of those women and I became very close friends, and our substantive conversations and collaboration as well as the laughter, lunches, and fun we shared, helped me understand why two of my Paulist confreres who had preceded me in ministry at the Newman Center had left the priesthood and married.

I, however, really wanted to be a priest and to do priests' work and to get myself as totally behind and into the ministry as I could. I knew that I had to pray and rely on God's grace to help me see that celibacy *is* possible and truly could be fulfilling. I was growing in my appreciation for the value of being single, feeling that I simply have to be one thing or the other with my whole heart, my whole strength, my whole attention. And to be totally dedicated to the Lord Jesus I would have to love him as a real person, and he would have to become my alpha and omega in all things.

It was clear to me that I must really commit myself to both prayer and to being a caring, genuine brother in community. And, in all things, to become more deeply spiritual, for the fulfillment sought would come through the inner senses of my interior life. My prayer was along the lines of "I do want to be a priest, Lord. Help me to engage at the deepest level in a more radical self-giving sense of commitment. Make me a priest to the core, Lord. May there be that experience of intimacy with you in my life. It's the ultimate experience the human heart is capable of."

I was enjoying the rich liturgical life, interactions with students and families, and our own community life. Then in the springtime came a "knock-knock" on my door from the Paulist leadership asking me if I would be open to moving to Montreal, Quebec, and directing the Newman Centre at McGill University.

I drove up to Montreal in the spring to have a look at the lay of the land—the university, the campus ministry offices, the city, and to talk with the Paulist who had already been working there for a few years in the Archdiocesan Office for Evangelization. He took me on a tour of what the archdiocese would now call the McGill Newman Centre—a large, four-story, stone house, with a small residence behind it, located on the edge of the university campus just a block or two in one direction from the heart of downtown Montreal, and in the opposite direction just a block-and-a-half from Mount Royal Park, a very large hill-park in the center of the city that gave the city its name in French, Montreal.

A tour of the upcoming Newman Centre facility left me with a sense that the building was in disarray and badly in need of repairs. Other realizations: overseeing ministry here would require one or two administrative staff persons as well as someone with maintenance skills. Life in the residence behind it would require cooking ability, and living in the largely French province of Quebec would require learning a new language.

That being said, I reflected that it could be good for me to be forced to learn to deal at least part of the time with what others have to deal with most of the time: budgeting and finances, and to develop more knowledge and skill in both. I presumed and genuinely welcomed the prospect of learning another language with the Paulist community's leadership providing the time, money, and support for it. Plus, there was already two lay candidates to work in administration there.

Deep down, I felt that I was ready for an assignment like this, and when I got back to Columbus, I sent an affirmative response to the Paulist leadership. And as summer approached, I decided to take a transitional month of vacation in July with friends, Bill and Cathie, who were enjoying a sabbatical year in Europe.

When I returned from that wonderful month, it was time to start saying good-bye to our worshipping community at Ohio State University, and to begin packing my bags for Montreal where another of my confreres, Fr. Ron Roberson, was also being assigned.

MONTREAL, QUEBEC

It was only after about a month in Montreal that I finally awoke without a great ache inside for all the friends whom I was missing in Columbus. A new morning rhythm and routine was emerging. I would generally enter the day with a run up the road on Mount Royal Park with a circle-around at the top and back down again. There was a good spirit of sharing among our community members back at the house. We enjoyed being together. Ron and I were not only chaplains but also the maintenance crew, working side-by-side in a home-life where everybody pitched in. A month seemed like a really short time for all of this to have come together in such a positive way.

At the Newman Centre, Ron and I were putting in place a schedule for weekend liturgies and encouraging students with musical talents to form musical groups and to animate our worship with music and song. It didn't take long before I was feeling energized and very invested in the ministry. As Christmas approached, we had a number of parties, and they accomplished their deepest purpose: to bring people together and expedite harmony and peace to all of goodwill. There was a lot of cross-fertilizing among different ethnic groups, musicians, and athletes. The sense of fun and level of sharing were remarkable.

As the new year approached, I took time to look back and evaluate this new assignment. The listing of "positives" was extensive:

good community life; convenient living quarters in a great location; good hiking and cross-country skiing; opportunity to learn another language, to test myself in a new leadership role, to grow in appreciation for the unique features of different ethnic groups, and to make new beginnings in peer friendships. I felt a sense of deep gratitude for the integrative wholeness between what I do and who I am. In short, I saw that my experiences fed my work, my preaching and counseling. Even the parties were a part of the ministry, as were the conversations on the way to and from ski outings. Prior to the students leaving for their homes and Christmas vacation, we had an Open House party. There was a wonderful spirit of sharing, with people enjoying very much just some time to be together. The students both worked hard and played hard! The sense of fun and level of sharing among my Paulist confreres was at an all-time high.

One of the ministerial programs I found most enriching to oversee at the Newman Centre was our marriage-prep program. The idea of marriage that struck me as so wonderful was that of two people basically committed to helping each other become their best selves. That, of course, is not "pure cake." The name of the game is communication, which is a synonym for "hard work." It takes a lot of strength and stamina, because if you're loving each other, you're growing, you're becoming, which is to say: you're changing. And that involves constantly telling each other who you *are*, what you're thinking and feeling *today*.

What really impresses me about a love relationship is that if two people are willing to work consistently at keeping the other up-to-date on what's happening in both their head (thoughts) and gut (feelings), the possibilities for growth are virtually endless. Would you say that there are many couples today who only mine a fraction of the gold in the mountain of their relationship because they're not willing to invest the time and energy in "swinging their pick" every day? Which is to say: communicating every day—risking, believing, trusting that the gold vein only gets deeper and wider the more energy you put into "swinging your pick."

One of the things I liked to say to the engaged couples in our marriage-prep program is that love is "yes" to you now, but it's also "yes" to you in the future. In a way, marriage is a big act of courage because you never know what's ahead. We don't like to dwell on misfortune, of course, but we have to admit it's a possibility that you might get hurt or sick. It's one thing to say, "I'm willing to deal creatively and courageously with what befalls me." But it's another thing to say, "I'm willing to love you and stay with you through whatever may happen to *you*." So really getting *married* to each other is a big order!

It's both helpful and important to have good models nearby whose lives say—"Hey, it can be done!" In letters I would receive from my mother, what came through is that being married is what and where she wanted to be more than anything else. The way that she referred to dad as "my beloved," or would tell me that "we had dinner by candlelight and wine when dad got home from work," or write that "I can't sleep when he's not home" all witnessed to the wonder and richness of love. For me it was a witness as well to how God loves us: faithfully, through thick and thin, through good times and bad. When, after years and years, the touch and kiss of your beloved still melts you, then you've experienced God who *is* love, and whose presence only gets deeper and warmer as we know and trust love more.

Chapter 2

PLANTING SEEDS FOR CHRISTIAN UNITY

When I was growing up in Minnesota—what Garrison Keillor liked to call "Lutherland"—I went to Catholic grade school and high school, and then to a Catholic College in New Jersey, and from there to teach in a Catholic high school in California. I never could have imagined when I entered the Paulist seminary a couple years later that my ministry after ordination would be in large measure devoted to unity among the followers of Jesus.

How did that come about? The Paulist Seminary was St. Paul's College in Washington, DC, and the various theological colleges in the area were linked together through the Washington Theological Consortium, which enabled seminarians or students in any one college to take courses in another. Some of the students at Lutheran Theological Seminary in Gettysburg, Pennsylvania, wanted to come to DC and benefit from this rich coalition of theological schools, but they needed a place to live. We had some available rooms at St. Paul's College and told them they were welcome to come live with us.

Although I was a Minnesota boy, I had never really had much personal contact with Lutherans, and now, all of a sudden, we were going to be *living together*! We lived on common corridors, enjoyed social time together in the communal living room before supper, shared three meals a day at common tables, used the same in-house library, shared resources with one another in our academic work, and occasionally had common prayer services as well. Needless to say, we got to know one another and relationships developed.

The experience of interdenominational life at St. Paul's College motivated me to extend my own range of ecumenical experience further through the Washington Theological Consortium. I went and lived and took a trimester of biblical studies at the Episcopal Seminary in Virginia, which gave me an opportunity not only to get to know some Episcopalian seminarians but to experience their prayer life with the *Book of Common Prayer* and other communal liturgies.

Getting to know brothers and sisters from other traditions of Christian faith, becoming familiar with and developing an experiential appreciation for both our liturgical commonalities and our distinctiveness felt right and good.

After my ordination to the diaconate in 1974, I was assigned to campus ministry at the Newman Center at Ohio State University in Columbus. I was delighted to discover that there was a Campus Ministers Association at OSU that provided opportunities to ministers from different denominations *to live their unity through ecumenical shared ministry*. Plus, a couple of those ministers didn't have offices on campus, and we had two available at the Newman Center that we offered them—so we were also literally engaging in our ministry from under the same roof!

One of the things I began doing each month was to invite students and their chaplain from other campus ministry centers to the Newman Center for an evening. One month it would be Lutheran students. The next month, Episcopalian students. The following month, students from the Methodist Center, then from the Presbyterian Center, and so on.

And when they would come to the Newman Center to engage with a gathering of Catholic students, they would be invited to share with us what they loved and found life-giving within their own tradition of Christian faith—a sharing that elicited questions from the Catholic students. Then we would invite the guest students to share any questions they might have about Catholics and their faith and practice. Needless to say, these forums engendered very rich and personal sharing between the students regarding their faith experience.

The marriage-prep program that I initiated at the OSU Newman Center also offered as one of its components an opportunity for couples to choose a workshop that would focus on a topic of particular interest to them. And one of these workshops was specially designed for interchurch couples. This is an offering that is even more needed today as the percentage of those couples marrying who are either interchurch or interfaith has grown by leaps and bounds, but I must also say that today when I hear of marriage-prep programs and inquire as to whether they offer something like a workshop for interchurch and/or interfaith couples to help them identify, discuss, and deal with certain situations and issues they will inevitably face, the answer is, unfortunately, "No, that is not part of our program."

Then, when I was transferred from the OSU Newman Center to the McGill University Newman Centre in Montreal, I saw that there were a couple more offices available than would be needed by our two Catholic chaplains, and soon learned that there were other denominational chaplains working on campus who did not have an office. So I made our offices available to them, and soon after, on one side of my office was now the office of the Presbyterian chaplain, on the other side was the office of the Christian Scientist chaplain, and the receptionist was Romanian Orthodox. As you might surmise, this facilitated regular communication among us and provided yet another opportunity to live our unity through ecumenical shared ministries on campus.

The archbishop of Montreal learned of my ecumenical "appetite" and further stirred it by appointing me as the English-speaking representative to the Montreal Council of Churches (yes, those were the days when such associations still existed in most cities!). On that Council was Fr. Irenée Beaubien, the Jesuit founder-director of the Canadian Centre for Ecumenism, the first post–Vatican II national Catholic Centre for Ecumenism in the world. We got to know one another, and about two-and-a-half years down the road, Irenée came to visit me one day at the Newman Centre.

"The position of assistant director is opening up at the Ecumenical Centre," he said, "and I'd like to invite you to apply for it." We talked for an hour and a half about the evolution of the Centre, and about his current assistant's declining health. When we finished, he said "Pray about it to discern if the Spirit is calling you to this ministry." I liked that approach of faith because, yes, I felt, that's what this must be—a decision of faith.

As I began to think and pray about it, I realized that accepting this ministry would mean staying in Montreal for years to come. Thoughts and questions then arose: "Would it be good to plant my feet in one place and take root? Montreal is a very stimulating city to live in. I have friends here. Why go somewhere new and start all over again? The multicultural (French/English) environment has been growing on me, and I've been finding it truly enriching. For the last four years I've felt drawn to ecumenical ministry, and there's no central office like this in the United States, and if there were, how would one become engaged with it?"

For me it's always been a value to go beyond where I am, to go on to new horizons, learn a new language, experience a new culture. Those have been big "pluses" for me, not something I'm interested in engaging in for just a few years and then back to "normal." That was likely one of the signs telling me I did have an ecumenical vocation. The ministry for unity requires one to be open to the "other"—the other's spirituality, culture, experience, and so on. It requires one to step out of what is "homey" and secure, and to experience something new in the context of "the other."

A door seemed to have opened in Fr. Beaubien's invitation. The surprise way it just sort of "popped out" bore the signature of God's way in my life. And the task at hand was to discern whether this inclination was actually from God. While all the other considerations above were real, some of them were not based on faith but on human likes and conveniences. So the core of the question was this: Is this where God is calling me? Because if it is, then I am going in that direction whether there seem to be any "fringe benefits" on the horizon or not.

Even at the early point in the process of discernment, there was something that felt "right" about it. I decided to consult the president of the Paulists and invite his input and that of the Paulist General Council. Their response was, "Christian unity is one of our community's mission objectives. We've been pleased to see your interest in giving this concrete expression in both Columbus and now Montreal. If you're being offered the opportunity to engage in this important gospel mission nationally in Canada, we are supportive of your applying for the position. You also have there a home you like with a couple Paulist confreres and a liturgical community at the McGill Newman Centre with which you have some roots, having served there as a chaplain the previous three years. You already have some friends there, a city you like, all those ecumenical contacts you already have there and a whole network to begin using."

In the recent Paulist General Assembly, the leadership had put out the message: "We need more specialists in the fields of Evangelization, Ecumenism, and Communications. We need more men in roles that are serving the wider church. We're getting too 'stuck' in parishes and Newman Centers—works that are traditional. Where is our charism to be breaking new ground?"

One of the Paulist ministries is preaching parish missions. I'd given some thought to preaching an ecumenical parish mission every now and then, but I saw more rootedness in working for the Canadian Centre for Ecumenism (CCE) than in just occasionally preaching, for example, ecumenical parish missions. In that, I would be moving around and just dealing with people in passing. But at the CCE, there would be much more opportunity for some consistent relationship with clergy in both my home diocese and dioceses further afield in other provinces. So I gave the go-ahead to our Paulist president to send a letter to Fr. Irenée Beaubien accepting his request for me to join the staff at the CCE.

As I looked down at the notebook on my desk, I saw the image of a vertical pole, and grasping onto that pole was a vaulter, "going for it." As I gazed on that image, I had the feeling that there was no more to say—just grab onto the pole and "go for it" with all the hope, effort, concentration, excitement, and adventure that the picture conveyed. As I looked at the picture, I saw the vaulter upended, vulnerable, not over-the-bar yet but going for it with everything he's got. There was no longer any "looking back." Now, I felt, it's all energy marshaled toward "upward" and "over."

Yes, it was "over"—the wondering, the discerning, the waiting, talking to people and weighing it out in letters and phone calls. My future now had a design upon it: the Canadian Centre for Ecumenism. I felt gratitude to the Paulist presidential board for their openness and willingness to look at this ministerial possibility, and for all the people who gave me their feedback and helped shape my own response.

I felt grateful that the Lord had led me to wonder after my meeting on June 1 with Fr. Beaubien whether this might be something I should look at seriously. It was now the end of October, and the wondering, waiting, discerning, talking to people was now over. My future had a new design upon it, and I felt gratitude for all the people who had given me their feedback and helped shape my response to what would now be a new chapter in my life.

At the end of the year (1979), one of the Catholic newspapers I was reading explicitly stated that "ecumenism is not a priority for the churches," a statement that made it clear that I was not going where the crowds are gathering, nor in the direction where the momentum is flowing. But another piece I read, in a quote from Mother Teresa of Calcutta, called me to pick up a pen and write her words down:

> Pray to be weak. It is not easy for us to accept weakness, but in this condition God works with us and works his will through us. In *strength* we try to direct our own lives. But in weakness, we let the Lord do the directing. This has been difficult for me to accept, but although I do not know where specifically I am being directed, I do know that the Lord keeps me weak enough to listen to him, then makes me strong enough to carry out his will.

These words had application for me as I prepared to work for unity among Christians. What can one do amid so many people, so many institutions, each with their own particular priorities and agendas? It can be challenging to even think of trying to have an impact.

Yet it is the Lord's work, and he was calling me to it. He had something in mind, some small contribution I could make. The more I could keep my own expectations out of it and just be guided by the Lord to accept what comes and doesn't come, the better I would be able to labor without discouragement, knowing that it is the Lord's plant and that he will give it growth in due season.

Chapter 3

YEAR OF BLESSING

As preparation for the ecumenical ministry in front of me, Fr. Beaubien wanted to give me the opportunity to deepen my knowledge *experientially* of other traditions in the Christian faith and gave me a year for preparatory studies and encounters. The prospect was before me of an exciting, challenging future that would begin with a year of learning in Europe and God-knows-where-else! I felt very much cast in the role of a pilgrim and knew I would have to travel lightly with my faith in the Lord as my support and guide to lead me and safeguard me.

This "training year" held the prospect of adventure, loneliness, wandering, challenge, fear, excitement, new friendships—all the things a pilgrimage holds. That was the spirit in which I would approach it: the spirit of a pilgrimage with my eyes upon the Lord, traveling lightly, living flexibly with utter dependence on God to support me in the journey.

ENGLAND: CANTERBURY ECUMENICAL SUMMER SCHOOL

I began with a study program titled "The Servants of God" at the Canterbury Ecumenical Summer School in England. Those whose teachings we were to survey were St. Augustine, St. Francis, St. Anselm, Martin Luther, John Wesley, Cardinal Newman, Karl Barth, and Teilhard de Chardin. The 162 participants from nine different countries were all Anglican save for twenty of us who came from half a dozen different denominations. Our common study of the Servants of God mentioned gave all of us the sense that our community is the Christian church. One of the greatest influences in making the church what it has been includes the lives and teachings of its leaders in the past.

A feature that drew me to this program was the opportunity for experiential learning. We had daily prayer with the Anglican *Book of Common Prayer*, opportunities for weekday Eucharist, and each Sunday went to a church representing a different branch within Anglicanism.

I had heard about the three main "parties" within Anglicanism—the "High Church" or Anglo-Catholic, the Low or Evangelical, and the Broad or Modernist, but had not had the opportunity to experience up close what that translated into in practice. It was an inductive learning experience, helping me understand that the Church of England and its North American counterpart embraced a wide spectrum of doctrine and practice.

The official name for it was "Anglican comprehensiveness," which is associated with the inclusion of both Protestant and Catholic elements in the one fellowship. Some of our participants described it as Catholic thesis, Protestant antithesis, and Anglican synthesis.

One of the things I enjoyed the most about the Canterbury Ecumenical Summer School was the opportunity for informal exchanges outside of the lectures. Such opportunities took place daily at what might be called the Anglican "holy hour"—afternoon tea with shortbread—or in the evening over a bottle of brew. As one of the participants reflected, "There's nothing like a few jars of ale to make all of us pub-stool theologians." Our conversations around the meaning of apostolic succession in the episcopate, the role of the Bishop of Rome, the criteria for who can be ordained, the understanding of real presence in the Eucharist, made us all give careful reading to the published agreed statements from the Anglican-Roman Catholic International Commission.

It was a rich and marvelous opportunity to better understand our unity so as to live it more fully. I remember asking an Anglican clergyman in a pub conversation one evening, "Do you think some kind of organic unity between our churches needs to wait until agreement on all those issues is reached?" His response I wrote in my journal before going to bed that night:

They've constructed the frame; now what we need are the plumbers and the electricians of unity—the practical people who can make what's on paper workable. That may be where we Anglicans have something special to contribute. We've never had a very tidy house. The way things go forward in the Anglican church baffles neatness and logic. That is the kind of spirit that needs to mark our move toward full communion—a willingness to keep things going forward even if every *t* is not crossed nor *i* dotted.

For all the mud in the face we Anglicans take on behalf of "comprehensiveness," it is precisely what enables us to reach out in different directions. It seems to me that there's a special vocation there to be an instrument for the restoration of visible unity. There have been many moments in the history of Anglicanism where there was a call to rule out one attitude or another, but the church has always chosen to endure the tension.

SWITZERLAND: THE ECUMENICAL INSTITUTE OF BOSSEY

After my summer in Canterbury, I traveled to Bossey, the Ecumenical Institute of the World Council of Churches located about twelve miles outside of Geneva, Switzerland. The centerpiece of its offerings at the time was a semester-long program called the Graduate School of Ecumenical Studies. There, in an eighteenth-century chateau lying in a tranquil plain between the Jura mountains and Lake Geneva, I found myself in a group of fifty-three students from thirty-five different countries and twenty-one different Christian denominations...and I was the only Roman Catholic! It was clear this was going to be for me an intense experience of "living unity." Over the next five months we would endeavor to live, study, pray, work, and play our way into an ecumenical community. My roommate was an Anglican deacon from Oxford, England.

Why had we come to Bossey? The goals of the graduate school told the story: to provide training for future generations of ecumenical leaders, both clergy and lay; to promote ecumenical theology within the context of intercultural and interconfessional encounters; to share in an ecumenical spirituality that respects the diversity of liturgical traditions; and to create a community in which ecumenism is experienced and shared.

The program involved two days of weekly lectures on the theme of "The Bible in the Life of the Church;" two days in seminar discussion groups; and a day each week at the World Council of Churches in Geneva, learning more about its work. Beyond that, our "ecumenical shared ministry" was to organize our life together. That included menus, liturgies, social life, dish washing, sports, cultural offerings, and desired academic supplements. We were being thrown into the pool and told to swim together. Filled with the air of idealism and good will, we would at least learn to "float" together.

Our liturgy committee worked on formats for prayer that would leave no one feeling completely out of his or her own element. It was not easy. Morning prayer succeeded. Vespers failed. A weekly Thursday evening Eucharist took root and became a regular feature with ministers from different churches presiding in a celebration of their own rite. On alternating Sundays, the various confessional families organized a liturgy according to their own tradition for the whole community.

There lurked under the cover of almost every event at Bossey some ecumenical shared experience and through it, potential learning and some broadening or deepening of vision. Our liturgy committee met, for example, to plan a retreat day. It seemed like a simple enough task. In my preceding years in campus ministry, I had planned numerous weekend retreats and wasn't expecting a great deal of difficulty in getting together with several others in the Bossey community to chart out a single day's format. Well, I soon learned that retreats may be standard practice in some Christian traditions, but by no means in all!

"What *is* a retreat?" the liturgy committee representatives of the Free and Reformed Church traditions wanted to know, and "What is it supposed to do? What are its components?" When I named "silence between the talks" as one of its components, Isaac, a Presbyterian from Ghana, said, "Silence? For one or two hours between talks? That is very strange! For my people a time of prayer means to gather together in church for a series of readings, songs, personal witness, and preaching."

I soon realized that the absence of monastic forms of life in Protestantism likely played a significant role in our different responses to silence. The retreat planning process took not one, not two, but several meetings, and in the end, the retreat was reduced to a four-hour period that opened and closed with structured half-hour prayer services, and with fifteen-minute sermons being offered in between every three-quarters of an hour. Only two-thirds of the people elected to participate in it.

There was no mistaking it: We were a mini-universe melted down, the universal church with all its variance of values and vision, and our life together at Bossey was a reality test for our ecumenical idealism.

But a couple months later, the retreat venue provided a very positive learning experience. When Christmas came, Daniel Ciobotea—an Orthodox theologian from Romania whose room was right next door to mine—and I decided to go to the Protestant Sisters' community of Grandchamp near Neuchatel, Switzerland, where there was going to be a retreat December 23–26.

THE COMMUNITY OF GRANDCHAMP

The community of Grandchamp is a women's monastic community that brings together sisters from different churches and various countries. About fifty sisters form the community, most of them living at Grandchamp, Areuse, in French-speaking Switzerland, with some living in the Netherlands and in France.

A little background to the community: In 1931, a sorority of faith had been born from the quest of a small group of Swiss Protestant women who began offering spiritual retreats. They were searching for a style of life that lent itself to prayerful listening to the Word of God. Their search led them to the monastic tradition, which, although rejected by the Reformers for its abuses and errors, was nevertheless in vibrant evidence in many places.

In the mid-1940s, the call to common life became clearer and the community became stronger in its vocation and began to develop. The first sisters returned to the sources of monastic life through the friendship and support of Anglican, Orthodox, and Catholic communities.

After World War II was over, women began to arrive from several European countries, drawn by what they had heard about a common life together that offered an equilibrium between contemplation and action. In 1952, seven of the sisters made lifetime commitments, and the sisters' community adopted the Rule of Taizé written by the Protestant Roger Schutz, who with some of his Protestant brothers just several years earlier had reintroduced monasticism into European Protestantism in southern France.

Both Taizé and Grandchamp, in forming their life of prayer and liturgy and service, have drawn from all the main traditions and both are wonderful examples of what "living unity and ecumenical shared ministry" looks like. At Grandchamp, Daniel and I experienced women from Churches of the Reform wearing a common habit, living a monastic life, singing the office, venerating icons, and celebrating the Eucharist twice weekly. Their openness to and integration of the spiritualities of East and West challenge both Orthodox and Catholics. How many of either of those two traditions have entered, by lived experience, into the deep emotions of Protestant consciences, for example, the Lutheran emotion of salvation through faith; the Calvinist awareness of the glory of God; and the Baptist and Methodist emotion of conversion?

Daniel's dissertation study had dealt with the integration of Eastern and Western forms of the Christian spiritual life. Topics relative to his studies and the subject of unity engaged us in conversation during many of our hours on the road.

"The solution for the course of unity that I see is this," Dan said in one of our conversations. "We must return to the essentials that we agreed upon in common and accept them anew. Anything that has been decided unilaterally or developed since then is not forced upon the other but is seen as proper to that tradition. For example, celibacy for the clergy. At one point, we agreed upon a common discipline for celibacy, but the West later made it mandatory for all," Daniel said. He continued:

> The Orthodox believe in the infallibility of the church and in the importance of a central figure of unity. They recognize from antiquity the primacy of the See of Rome. But Rome, being the only patriarchal See in the West after the schism, developed in the direction of a monarchy, while the Oriental and Orthodox churches preserved the accent of conciliarity. Each one needs to an extent what the other has. The West needs to give more autonomy to the local churches. The Eastern churches—who have developed so

> deeply in the direction of autonomous national churches to the point that it is a problem among themselves—need a stronger leader and office of unity.

Today, Dan Ilie Ciobotea is the Patriarch of the Romanian Orthodox church.

Back at Bossey, our ecumenical community soon boarded a bus for a weekend at Taizé, just a few hours away in southern France.

FRANCE: THE COMMUNITY OF TAIZÉ

Our midwinter visit to Taizé revealed some Protestant/Catholic differences. Taizé is an ecumenical monastic community with regular times for prayer on a daily basis. The nature of these prayer services, however, affected members in our Bossey group differently given our various denominational backgrounds.

Some found there to be a lack of variety in the character of the services, for example, the candle lighting and mood of evening vespers was the same as that for the Sunday morning Eucharist. The absence of preaching in the Service of the Word was reacted to. Africans in our group had never heard the office sung, and since this is the core of Taizé's daily prayer, they felt quite uncomfortable at the daily office services. "Is this what ecumenism is about—syncretism?" one of them asked.

The church at Taizé impressed some like a womb: dark, silent, secure, with people sitting or kneeling in fetal positions. "Does the prayer here take us toward interdependent maturity or backward toward self-centered infantilism?" asked another in our Bossey group. Many of our group members sat around the periphery during the services. It seemed to be body language for "I want to be here, but on the fringe where I can kind of stand outside it and watch it. I'm not going to be manipulated by the mood of these lights and get sucked into this."

Was the reaction of our group so critical and uncomprehending because most of them were Protestants, revealing that the monastic life and worship style of Taizé are more "Catholic" in their form and expressions? Or were they reacting to what they were simply not accustomed to and, therefore, didn't understand? The reactions of some in our group did make me more aware of the Catholic character of our Taizé experience. When we see something we're not accustomed to, our response is one of reserve, caution, suspicion, and we feel put off by its strangeness. This was the response I saw among many of our group members.

In addition to participating in their rich experience of chanting and prayer three times a day, we had the opportunity to meet the brothers and enjoyed a "Q & A" session with Brother Max Therian, one of Europe's most respected theologians at the time. I was struck by his own emphasis on grassroots ecumenism.

"Taizé," he said, "doesn't want to be a movement or a place of pilgrimage. It wants to inspire and encourage involvement on church local levels. It wants to motivate people who come here from different countries to share with one another what they are doing to promote Christian unity back in their home countries, to motivate them to cross-fertilize one another. Taizé does not want people to focus on *this place* but on *their local situations*."

GREECE: MOUNT ATHOS

After the five-month experience at Bossey of "living unity," I journeyed from Western Europe to Greece and Egypt for some up-close experience of life in Orthodox and Oriental monasteries and parishes.

Mount Athos is a forty-mile-long promontory that stretches into the Aegean Sea in northern Greece. It was an area eminently suited to those wishing to practice the rigors of an ascetic life, and from the earliest years of the Byzantine period it attracted men from all parts of the Empire. Today, there are about twenty monasteries built near the cliff all around the peninsula. I stayed in four of them.

Athos is considered by many the cradle of Orthodoxy and is known as the Holy Mountain. Those who have chosen to live there find relative seclusion and isolation from the inquisitive outside world for the pursuance of their monastic aims. It has resisted infiltration by any Western influence.

One of the ways this found expression was that, if the monks in a monastery where I was staying came to know that I was a Catholic priest, when it came time for their prayer services, they would direct me just to sit in the vestibule in the back and watch.

EGYPT: ST. MACARIUS

When I went to Egypt, my first destination was the ancient Coptic monastery of St. Macarius, situated in the desert between Cairo and Alexandria. It was founded in the year 360 by Macarius who tutored more than four thousand monks of different nationalities.

Arriving in the evening, I knew I was in for another fresh experience when I was led to my monastic cell by one of the monks who handed me a candle and some matches, and said, "At three in the morning the waking bell will call the monks to prayer for an hour in their cells. At 4 a.m. you will hear a second bell calling everyone to hymn-chanting in the chapel." Indeed, the next morning at 4 a.m., thin, burning tapers revealed black-robed, cowled figures sitting on the floor or against the chapel walls, chanting.

It was Lent, and it soon became clear that fasting is practically a sacrament for the Copts. They fast 180 days per year. During Lent, they eat just one meal a day. They see the demise of fasting in the West as decadence and loss of spiritual values. Is it any wonder that, since my time in Egypt, I have written two books encouraging the recovering of fasting in our Western practice?[1] Another thing that really impressed me was that each day the monks recite all 150 psalms—by heart!

My growing passion for Christian unity was encouraged by a conversation with the spiritual father of the monastery, Matta El Meskeen, who had written on the theme. "The church is the new creation," he said, "and Christ is the only one who can fill it. His body is a source of life and unification, capable of abolishing all sorts of barriers created by time and place, whether social, cultural, sexual, or religious. The church, by nature of its catholicity, is against all sorts of division and isolation. It is only when people earnestly surrender their lives to Christ that the life of Christ, which is one and undivided will be manifested in the church, his body. How," he asked, "is it going to be proved to the world that God is one but through the oneness of those born from him?"

ISRAEL: JERUSALEM

Toward the end of Lent, I went to Jerusalem to experience the liturgical richness contained within the church universal. It was a year in which the Western Holy Week and Eastern Holy Week were back-to-back. After soaking up the wonderful liturgies in Western churches, I obtained a master schedule of all the services for Orthodox Holy Week. Two acquaintances and I put together a plan whereby we would spend every morning, afternoon, and evening in a different Divine Liturgy. For the next three days we would literally "live in church"!

I was struck by how "at home" the Orthodox Christians were in their church—moving about, lighting candles, kissing icons, touching everything. Between services in the Church of the Holy Sepulcher, I watched the faithful people kneel before the marble slab that lies midway between Calvary and the tomb, in memory of the anointing of Christ's body before burial. They would anoint the stone with aromatic balms, rub their hands over the slab and then rub their own face and neck and hair with the transferred ointment, place their cheeks to the stone with great tenderness and closed eyes, soak up the sacred balm with any available cloth and then reroll it so as to take it back home to a family member or friend who could not make the pilgrimage.

My friends and I reflected on the richness of the Eastern rites. Day after day we emerged from three-hour liturgies in which we didn't even understand the language, but all we could say when we came out was that we had been "filled up!" When one considers that all the Eastern liturgical rites predate the schisms that divided Christianity, they testify to an admirable unity-in-diversity within the one church and are a meeting place where all the churches today can rediscover their apostolicity.

It is a consolation to pray—to learn how to pray—in union with Christian brothers and sisters from whom we are in some way separated. As we wait and work and pray for the reunion of Christians, these rites and our familiarity with them are like so many bridges that have not been destroyed and offer us a way of meeting, getting to know one another better, praying together, and, yes, *living our unity.*

Chapter 4

RETURN TO CANADA

When I got back home to Montreal after this "Year of Blessing," I began planting seeds for unity among Christians in the ten provinces of Canada. My focus was on local-level initiatives. When I would be invited to the different provinces for a conference or to preach at a worship service, I would also ask the local leaders if they would organize a session in which I could meet and talk with interchurch couples. It was clear the couples really appreciated the opportunity to meet one another and share how they were dealing with the various questions they uniquely faced. In some towns and cities, the groups began to meet at regular intervals to share and support each other in their journeys. In time, the Canadian Association of Interchurch Families evolved.

I was only just beginning a full-time ministry for Christian unity. If anything, I was surprised at how content I felt to settle into a pattern of reading, writing, meetings with occasional talks, trips, and preaching. It was both challenging and stimulating to go on to new horizons, learn a new language, experience a new culture. They were all "pluses" for me, and I took that as one of the signals telling me I really did have an ecumenical vocation. The ministry for unity requires one to be open to the other—the other's spirituality, culture, and experience. It requires one to step out of what is "homey," secure, and to experience the reality of "the other." My perception was that I was "wired up" in such a way as to be stimulated by the kinds of experiences that this ministry would send my way.

The strength of our ecumenical work at the Canadian Centre for Ecumenism lay in our freedom to initiate new projects and to share what we learned from them. Consultations with interchurch and interfaith couples. Summer Ecumenical Institutes. Interfaith Institutes. Ecumenical parish missions. Ecumenical and interfaith dialogues. Our quarterly periodical *Ecumenism*.

The work, however, soon became unrelenting. My desire was for an ordered life that was not characterized by rush nor by always being late because I was trying to do too many things. It was proving challenging to protect space in the schedule for some leisure time for prayer, community, exercise, and reading.

Our staff team and the combination of elements in the work at the CCE made it a stimulating and satisfying ministry, but given it was the ministry of a national office there was always just too much to do. We set some priorities with the objective in mind of limiting the number of things we would try to respond to, but it didn't work. An example of the kind of projects that would "pop up": I'd been looking at March as the month when I could catch up on three weeks of accumulated dossiers and the pile of things on my desk to read through and deal with. Then along came the director, Irenée, with a new project: fourteen television programs that we were to plan and oversee, and he wanted to divide them equally among three of us.

What I needed to be able to do in those situations was say, "It's a worthy project, but I'm already in 'overload' and not in a position to help out on it." But setting limits was not one of my strong points. When Fr. Beaubien retired after my first three years on the Centre staff and handed off the Centre Director's baton to me, the challenge of finding balance in the workload would only increase.

INNER NUDGES

Over the course of my fourteen years at the Canadian Centre for Ecumenism, one of the things I saw was the need for places where Christians could come together for longer periods of time to share faith and get to know one another better. When a marvelous property and chateau-like home at the foot of Mount Royal in the middle of the city became available, a light when on. It had served as the founding location by Benedictines John Main and Laurence Freeman of what is now the World Community of Christian Meditation in France.

The archbishop was looking for how best to make good use of this mansion now available, and as his ecumenical officer I proposed that he make of it an ecumenical center for spirituality, cosponsored by the different churches in the city. He had been praying over this, too, and had asked four religious communities to join their prayers to his own. Our visions resonated strongly with one another on all the essential points: a place where people learn how to pray in new ways; ecumenical participation; a residential community of ecumenical composition, women and men, French and English. We found ourselves very much in the same wavelength. To make a long story short, he liked the idea and told me to organize an evening with supper at and a tour of the mansion for the various denominational church leaders in the city.

They were impressed by what they saw and gave a ready nod to the proposal that we make it an ecumenical center for spirituality with retreats, workshops, and programs for all the churches. When the archbishop and I met again in follow-up, he shared that he'd been thinking about who he might ask to take on this project and that my ecumenical background, interest in the spiritual life, and bilingual capability made me someone in whom he could have trust. I felt like a "marked man" now, someone sleepwalking toward a cliff. Subconsciously he knows the terrain, but he is pulled toward the edge by an undefinable force and feels unable—unwilling even—to resist taking one step after another, aware that there is an edge not far away where he will lose control and go into free fall.

My own clarity about where the Spirit was calling me was not strong enough at that point to support more than tentative exploration. We had just completed a successful fundraising drive at the CCE, the team was working well together, and there were many more projects and possibilities there than I could handle. The question that lurked within me was: What am I doing laying the groundwork for something that could very possibly take me away from the Centre? Turning this wonderful mansion into an ecumenical center for spirituality could take on a life of its own!

My prayer was, "Lord, I need you to be very clear with me: if this is where you want me to go, then let me know. I will not cling to where I am at the Ecumenical Centre. I will go where you want me to go and do what you ask of me. But this I ask of *you*: if this is from you, let me know it. I cannot go forward with any conviction as long as I am unsure of this."

Not long after, I met again with the archbishop and his team. When we discussed the finances of it, the finance officer's response was "I'm not worried about the money aspect. If this is from the Holy Spirit, the money will come." Outside his office afterward, standing by the elevator, the archbishop commented, "So far, so good," and let me know that he, too, had felt the movement of the Spirit with regard to the mansion.

I was however happy at the CCE. We were in a better position financially than at any time in my directorship, and the team was working very well together. But as a friend said, "What the Spirit may be moving you toward will only be an extension of the work you're doing now; not something totally other or different." And through all this I felt an inner, gentle nudging to just keep taking the "next step."

Chapter 5

UNITAS

That inner spiritual intelligence led me to put the word out to the Canadian Centre for Ecumenism's Board of Directors that, after working at the CCE for fourteen years and serving as its director for twelve of those years, I felt my time was drawing to a close.

It was a leap of faith to undertake the huge task of developing a stable infrastructure for the soon-to-be-established ecumenical center for spirituality, and to put the whole operation on a firmer footing. Beyond the marvelous mansion itself, we were very poor in human and material resources, and the decisions and challenges in front of us made me cower and cringe just thinking about them.

Yet, the Holy Spirit seemed to be steadfastly supporting me in putting my shoulder to the wheel and giving myself entirely to this effort. That said, it was nonetheless an act of faith. I was leaving all to follow that call: My appreciable community life with two Paulist confreres. My work and colleagues at the Ecumenical Centre.

But the way the new house was already being used encouraged me to take the next step. In the coming weekend there would be the Anglicans participating in their synod; the French Presbyterians on an away-day together; and the French Catholics in a meditation retreat. Our being together in the same place was itself a positive witness. People met and talked, relationships were created, collaboration grew. Such happenings are all part of the ecumenical project, and there needs to be places where such can happen. We decided to name the place Unitas (Latin, for Unity). In 1995, I left my role as director of the Canadian Centre for Ecumenism and Unitas became my new home and ministry.

Within a year, Unitas was up and running, cosponsored by eight different denominations. It was grassroots ecumenism at its best. Within five years we had 9,000 participants annually in our seminars, workshops, and retreats. Clearly, it responded to a need.

I felt gratitude and excitement about Unitas being my new matrix, about the opportunities to shape it and live it. And the wisdom of a new life rhythm at Unitas soon became manifest as well. The quiet, trees, garden, communal meditation, more casual dress—all worked together to move us away from priorities of doing, wanting, having toward the priority of *being*: the sweet spot of life! I put up a hammock between two trees in the backyard, which soon afterward gave birth to a poem:

> Floating in mid-air on a hot August afternoon,
> recording a warbler's full-throated song,
> rocking to 'n fro in an envelope of ether,
> arms and legs dangling like a man in free fall.
> Looking at the world upside-down through eyes half-closed,
> kaleidoscopic patterns of light dance on my lashes as I'm
> smiling at the canopy of pine branches spread protectively
> above,
> feeling securely held and enfolded in a gentle embrace,
> swimming ever nearer to the sweet spot of life.

But while I had arrived at a sweet spot of bliss in this new residence, I had not downshifted my level of activity in years past—the desire for which was a large part of my reason for coming to this new engagement. Due to my engagements on the road, for example, I was still not in a rhythm of life that allowed the time for the spiritual reading, exercise, and time with friends that I desired. My morning reading time was being eaten up by work-related project preparation, and there simply wasn't enough time in the normal workday to both respond to the administrative stuff at Unitas *and* prepare my talks for road retreats, so I ended up using daily morning and evening hours for the latter. I eventually decided the only way for me to find the rhythm I wanted was just to stay home more. I hadn't gotten into the rhythm of life I wanted to find at Unitas, and it had everything to do with my engagements on the road.

As we headed into a new year at Unitas, my resolve was to (1) do less; (2) leave larger spaces between what I do so as to prepare calmly and without undue pressure; (3) have more time *for* and *with* people. One of the reasons I wanted to step out of my job at the

CCE and come to Unitas was to be *less* busy and have more time for *people*. My prayer was "Slow me down, Lord. I want to enjoy living in this beautiful place and connecting with the people who come here. The answer lies with me. I am doing it to myself, and I can change it. A couple things I think are important for my spiritual growth: To relax more, laugh more, and to enjoy more time with others."

Once I began making some progress in establishing that rhythm, there came yet another new development. In 1998, the president of the Paulists, Fr. Frank Desiano, came up to Montreal and visited me at Unitas to ask if I would leave what I was doing and open and develop the work of a Paulist North American Office for Ecumenical and Interfaith Relations. "We like the work you're doing," he said, "but you're doing it under somebody else's shingle (the Canadian Centre for Ecumenism and then Unitas). We'd like you to do it under the Paulist shingle because we want to be more clearly associated with this work in the eyes of the church. This is an important part of our mission, and the community wants to give a clearer and more visible sign of that."

A few months later, the Paulist General Assembly passed a resolution to establish a Paulist National Office for Ecumenical and Interfaith Relations. There was a session for break-out groups to discuss "how we can more effectively animate our ecumenical ministry." Each group came back with a recommendation for the Assembly to establish an office/officer/coordinator first of all for us as a community, and then for our relationships with other churches and ecumenical agencies. That evening, the Presidential Board responded with the plan for a coordinator for intra- and extramural relationships with a pastoral ministry in the area of spirituality. I heard this mandate/call from the community's leadership with the intuition that there would soon be a knock on my door.

The job description reflected in large measure my ministry at the Canadian Centre for Ecumenism, albeit with a different constituency—Paulists and American churches, organizations, and networks. When I talked with our president about it and asked, "Who are you looking to in the community to fulfill this role?" his response was, "I'm looking to you! You can help the community get the ecumenical dimension of its mission more solidly in place. Are you ready to move on this now, to set the wheels in motion?" We discussed how to proceed, given my present leadership role at Unitas, and agreed that 1999 would be my final year there.

A week later, sitting on the wonderful balcony at Unitas and looking out over the city of Montreal, I found myself somewhat amazed at the tranquility of spirit I was feeling within. The transformation that was occurring within was mysterious and all I could say is that the timing felt right and that inner doors had opened, and I was walking through them peacefully even though I had only a vague idea of what would be in the "next room." The community's leadership had agreed to give me a final year at Unitas and to find new leadership there to whom I could hand off the baton. After twenty-two years in Canada in local, regional, and national ministries, coming back to the States would be a challenging process in a variety of ways.

I was, however, feeling increasing readiness to return to the States and to live in a Paulist community again. I still wanted to do retreat work in an ecumenical context but sought to be relieved of the administrative burdens of running a spirituality center. The work I desired to do: preaching, workshops, seminars, retreats, and writing. The desire was there to carry this ministry into a new expression with more freedom to actually *do* the aspects of it that I really love. Our president Frank assured me that this was something the Paulist community saw a need for and assured me that it was going to happen.

In 2000, I returned to the United States to found and develop a Paulist North American Office for Ecumenical and Interfaith Relations, which was located for its first seven years in New York City, and after that, seven years in Washington, DC, followed by six years in Boston where there is—thanks to the movement called UniteBoston—joint prayer services, shared religious music concerts, and a growing grassroots network of Christians meeting in each other's homes for neighborhood suppers and developing relationships with one another.

I was, of course, concerned that Unitas's future not be jeopardized by this evolution, but I had to trust that if the Holy Spirit who called me into it was now calling me out of it, that the Spirit would see to new leadership stepping forward to carry things ahead. I knew that the breaking of this news and the year of farewells that lay ahead would have its difficult moments, but I was ready to live that.

The Unitas mansion was aging, and increasingly in need of some significant repair, the money for which we did not have. In January 1999, a meeting of church leaders approved motions instructing the

Unitas Board of Directors to begin looking for a new building for Unitas, and they pledged that money from the sale of the building would be in support of programming and staff salaries in the new location.

I was stunned and in a state of shock. I felt as though I had just been informed that a close friend or family member had died and sat there numbly trying to comprehend what I had just heard. Why should it feel like this? Because in the logistical nightmare of leaving this place, and finding another as well as a new director, there was such a strong likelihood that people who otherwise would have stayed together had the center remained stable, would now scatter, and that there would be a period of interval in which everything we had built up and painstakingly created from house culture and ethos to a network of friends and supporters, would likely be lost. I could see it unfolding, and it felt like a death—the death and dissolution of a dream, the coming apart of five years of intensive work and prayer. There was a verse in the day's scripture reading (Sir 2:1–11) that was timely: "My child, when you come to serve the Lord, prepare yourself for trials. Set your heart and be steadfast, for gold is tested in the fire."

My prayer was, "Lord, help me as I grapple and absorb this experience of death. Surely there have been countless others who invested years of their lives in causes they believed in only to see them founder and fail through political events or natural disasters or want of funding. Help me believe that you can work through all circumstances to advance your reign in our hearts. Teach me valuable truths through this experience. Cultivate God-like qualities of patience, compassion, faith, and hope in me through these events."

As time went on, in reading one day the *Testimony of St. Paul* by Carla Martini, I was very struck by her observation that after being knocked from his horse and being personally, directly visited by the Lord, Paul did not rush into mission and begin preaching. He spent the next ten years of his life in obscurity and difficulty and only began to speak and write about the experience fourteen years after it took place. During that time, the Lord continued the work of purification in him, emptying his heart of all personal achievements so that he might become more and more a versatile instrument in the hands of God, softening his personality and preparing him for his mission.

I could relate to that. It was what seemed to be happening to me. Unitas was a sign of my personal achievement in the past six years, and it was all going. Maybe to another place in another expression. Maybe nowhere. Maybe it was finished. All I could say was, "You are Lord. This is your work and you're in charge. I've tried to be a versatile instrument in your hands here these past six years, leaving the security of my position at the CCE to make myself available to you for this project. And now I ask you to help me not cling to it, not fight what is happening, but simply to serve in whatever way you would like me to."

As my time to return to the United States drew near, the Paulist president proposed we locate our new national office for ecumenism in New York City, the home of our founder Fr. Isaac Hecker and of our "mother church," St. Paul the Apostle.

While on retreat that year, I reflected on twenty-five years of priesthood, and listed a number of surprises:

- At the time of my ordination, I had never even been outside of North America.
- I never thought 90 percent of my first twenty-five years of ministry would be in Canada.
- I never foresaw 80 percent of my ministry being ecumenical and interfaith.
- I never dreamed I would have the opportunity to see as much of the world as I've seen.
- I never foresaw learning, living, and working in another language (French).
- I always liked to write but didn't foresee writing books as part of my ministry.
- Having been born and raised in a small rural town in southern Minnesota, I certainly never saw myself living in midtown Manhattan.

Part Two

BACK TO THE UNITED STATES

Chapter 6

NEW YORK CITY

The new Paulist Office for Ecumenical and Interfaith Relations was located at St. Paul the Apostle Church in New York City, our mother church founded by Fr. Isaac Hecker, founder of the Paulist Fathers. The parish is located in mid-town Manhattan, a block and a half from mile-long Central Park on the east side and about three blocks from a bike trail along the Hudson River on the west side, to say nothing of all the museums, theatres, monuments, and shops in downtown Manhattan.

All the Paulist community members in the house gathered for a blessing and dedication of the office and seemed appreciative and supportive of this ministry. We followed it with hors d'oeuvres in the living room of the house. I felt good about the beginning of my sojourn there.

A few days later, I was off to preach an ecumenical parish mission in Nova Scotia, Canada. It was the kind of "hands-on" ecumenical work I enjoyed most, the kind that impacts the lives of people in real ways, in positive ways, in transformational ways. It doesn't matter where the people are: big cities, small towns—people are people. This particular mission served as a trampoline sending me in the direction of reactivating ecumenical parish missions.

From there I went to our seminary, St. Paul's College, in Washington, DC, for Hecker Day festivities celebrating the life and ministry of our Paulist Founder, Isaac Hecker. I was delighted to have about ten days there, being more at the heart of the community's life. And oh-so-grateful that the concerns of house and staff and money were off my back, and I could just stay there and work for three days between the Hecker events and the beginning of the upcoming Evangelical workshop in DC. I felt very grateful for all the blessings of fellowship, community, and ministry.

On another front, the ministry in the new Paulist national office was taxing from the get-go because I had no help and had to do everything myself. So when I was on the road as required by the ministry, mail, email, financial documents would all accumulate, keeping me in the office until late at night once I got back. The workaholic pattern started creeping back in....

The events that took me on the road, however, were enriching. I began visiting our Paulist parishes and campus ministry centers, engaging in dialogue with my confreres and their staff about their opportunities for ecumenical engagements and collaboration in their ministries. A favorite topic in my conversations with them was "spiritual ecumenism" as the heart of the movement: prayer together; personal, communal, and ecclesial conversion; and the exchange of spiritual gifts.

A good example of this was a two-day conference at the Oversees Ministry Study Center now located in Princeton, New Jersey. I returned happy and energized by spending time with about sixty Evangelicals, a group with whom I had little direct experience of any depth. I was deeply impressed by the quality of the people who came together from the United States, Canada, England, and even Cyprus. Impressed by their erudition, prayerfulness, faith, and welcome to me, the only Catholic participating.

The presenters were excellent, but even more valuable for me than their reflections on conversion and repentance was observing their own dynamics and ethos as Evangelicals. I am no stranger to the ways of prayer, but they prayed in a way that I had never witnessed before. I cherish that kind of "crossing-over encounter" and the way it opens me up to new riches in the spiritual life. I came back feeling ready to make time in my schedule again for those in this tradition of Christian faith. It felt like discovering a new, more remotely related branch of the family, and wanting to get to know them better.

At one of the Prayer Services, we were invited to enter into an inner personal dialogue with Jesus. And I was indeed struck by what I heard Jesus saying to me: "You tend to feel you have to work really hard at things before they'll happen. But sometimes your strenuous efforts get in the way and block the process that will bring it about nicely in due time. So relax more. Let go and let the Holy Spirit guide you."

As I sat there and reflected, I began to take some notes on what I was hearing within:

1. Fast from office work in the evenings. What I hear God saying is "Don't allow yourself to be worn down by overwork. This does not glorify me. This is counterproductive. Stay peaceful and vitalized at your center. Take your evenings for drinking from the wells of spirit that feed you." When I pictured myself working days but having evenings free, I felt a surge of energy, and my being said "Yes!"
2. Freshening up relationships: each week put in a call to friends, or relatives with whom you have only infrequent contact.

Overall, as I looked back on this ministry, I become aware of some of its effects on me. I was feeling very affirmed in this "calling," in this role/ministry. The work of the past month had required me to do some integrative work both personally and theologically. Leading theological reflection sessions with our parish staff was enriching both for them and for me.

In that feeling affirmed, there was an experience of the zone of liberty within me expanding. It's like when any person feels very confirmed in who they are and what they're doing, the person becomes more deeply at ease in his/her skin, and relates to people from that grounded, confident place within. The regular ministry of preaching in very different settings has also been good for me. Getting to know my confreres better has been good. Renewing my acquaintance with the West Coast has been good.

The prayer that surfaced within me: "I am feeling very blessed, Lord. Thank you for the privilege of serving you in this way. Thank you, Holy Spirit, for using me, for working through me in these various situations. Continue, everywhere and at all times, to use me to sow seeds of unity and understanding."

Another enriching gathering was a three-day National Convocation for Evangelization in Louisville, Kentucky. It put diocesan ecumenical officers and directors of evangelization in dialogue with one another in a series of stimulating sessions. This conference was like a crowning jewel, representing in an institutional way what I'd been about on the local level with Paulists: working the fit between dialogue and proclamation in our church's understanding of evangelization.

I had some apprehension about how my own presentation on the interreligious implications of Catholic evangelization would "land" with this group of largely diocesan directors of evangelization, but in my final going over of the text, and then in delivering it, I just had a calm sense of "This is where our church is at, and all I need to do is to present it and let it speak for itself." And it did. Precisely because what I said was rooted in church documents, people listened up and appreciated it. As one said afterward, "I felt really stretched and stimulated." Both Bishop Blair from Stockton, California, the chair of the Bishops Commission for Ecumenism and Interreligious Relations, and Bishop Slattery from Tulsa, Oklahoma, made a beeline for the speaker's podium at the end of the session to express their thanks. During the break, many others came to say how helpful they had found our session and to inquire where they could get a copy of my presentation to take home.

Then, in the closing session, the speakers were brought together at a table in the front of the hall to respond to questions from any of the participants. There were some basic questions that surfaced, like "Are we to try to bring our Protestant friends into the Catholic Church or not?" and I found myself in the role of respondent. Once again, directors of evangelization came up afterward and expressed their appreciation for my "systematic and clear" responses. "I wish I could just take you home with me," the diocesan director in Baltimore said, "and have you talk with everyone I work with." When I came in and sat down next to Dr. Margaret Ralph (who's written nine books in the area of scripture) for the closing liturgy, she said, "I've learned more from you than from anyone here during these days. You have a gift for going straight to the point and saying something clearly that not everybody has said. I'm feeling very grateful toward you right now."

Before going to bed that night, I shared this with the Lord in my journal:

> Lord, as I listened to these affirmations, I felt confirmed in my ministry; felt you really using me and all the experiences both ecumenical and interreligious that you have given me over the years. This feedback does not feed the false self; it helps my true self, rooted in you, to recognize the gifts that are there. We never know ahead of time that what we have to share will in fact be valued and appreciated until in fact we learn that it is. What happens inside me is a deep sense of "I'm in the right place. I'm doing what you want me to be doing, Lord, and the integration that has happened inside me through all the experiences you have given me over the years is being put at the service of your people in ways I could never have foreseen—like being given a mandate to go to all Paulist foundations in the country to help them shape their vision of ministry, and to speak at national gatherings like this one."

What I saw through the sessions of this entire month was that the integration of perspectives I'd been working with of Dialogue and Proclamation as partner expressions of Evangelization represents something fresh and new for people, a liberating, direction-giving map of the way forward at a time of dizzying complexity. I felt energized in "connecting the dots" and working through this integration within myself, and I was grateful for the opportunity to share it with both evangelists and ecumenists—bishops, clergy, and laity alike—and hear back from them that it was very helpful in making clearer the mission of the church in our time. My consistent prayer: "Thank you, Holy Spirit, for giving light and showing the way."

In Cardinal Walter Kasper's book *That They All May Be One*, there is repeated iteration that spiritual ecumenism is the heart of the ecumenical movement: prayer; personal, communal, and ecclesial conversion; and the exchange of spiritual gifts. These things have been my path. Because it has been an intensely personal path as well as an ecclesial ministry, I have been able to avoid becoming an "ecumenical bureaucrat" or professional functionary in a job.

I liked living in our parish neighborhood of New York City very much. Having a parish in which I could minister as a priest was wonderful and was a good source of friendships. My office quarters were ideal, and the network of offices it made most sense for me to be working with were there in the city, to say nothing of other "positives" like Central Park or the bike trail along the Hudson, Lincoln Center and Broadway. In terms of the work the community was asking me to do, I personally believed that the decision we made in 1999 to locate this office in New York City was a good one and that this was indeed the best place for me to advance the work.

Seven years later in 2007 came the call to go to Washington, DC, occasioned by the renovation of our seminary there, St. Paul's College. Part of the plan involved creating a wing of the building to be called the Hecker Center for Ministry that would house the Paulist national ministries. I had followed the Spirit's urgings in leaving Montreal and coming to New York City. My assessment of the years that I spent in New York City is that they had been perhaps more fruitful and marked by a deeper inner peace and emotional tranquility than any other tantamount stretch of my life as a priest. That being said, I trusted that in DC, where the national Council of Churches is located, there would be new networks, new advantages, new friendships, and new opportunities for ministry that I would discover.

Once again, I recognized that this would be a prime time for "spiritual practice," and that the next year of transition would be replete with opportunities for practicing letting go, spiritual dying, not-clinging. I sought to live these moments consciously and to grow in spiritual freedom through the process, once again discovering that every new experience of life only comes through an experience of letting go, of dying. It was once again time to "walk my talk," living each step of the process with awareness.

After learning about this impending move from the Paulist president, I went up into the chapel and prayed the prayer of Charles de Foucault: "Lord, I abandon myself into your hands. Help me to be ready for all, to accept all. Let only your will be done in me and in all your creatures. I ask no more than this, O Lord. I surrender myself to you without reserve and with complete confidence, for you are my Savior."

When we are living out of our gifts and calling, the energy is given. That energy is an uncreated energy that is coming from God. It is not just an external gift *from* God, but *is* God's very being divinizing us, transforming us from within and making our hearts beat with God's own passion and energy and love. Holding things in balance is a constant struggle, requiring incessant readjustment to the circumstances of each week. The important thing is not to do it all or even do it right; just to do it with faith and love.

I resolved to enjoy my last weeks in the Big Apple, New York City. There was a mellow party for me, and I did some pleasurable things. One of my confreres and I went to see the film *Into Great Silence*. I walked over to Lincoln Center for *La Traviata* at the Met and took in a new exhibit there as well on Islam and Venice. Went out for supper (not something I did very often in this city of restaurants) with a friend at The Rock Center Café right next to the skating rink at Rockefeller Center. Given that it was springtime, we were surprised to see people still skating! We enjoyed a delicious meal and over dessert, the manager, who my friend knew, came by and chatted and tossed out an encouraging word to take to the rink, which I of course jumped at! The manager returned with two complimentary tickets worth $45 for skate rentals and rink entry. We skated in spring temps for forty-five minutes. It was really fun—all the more so for being such an unexpected delight! I took it as a wink of unexpected things to come in DC.

The inspiration to leave after Easter was "right on." Lenten spirituality supported the inner process of letting go, saying good-bye, and looking gratefully at the blessings of my years in New York City. The time I allowed for packing was just right, too. My plan was to be ready to go by Thursday eve, and then give myself over to the Triduum's inner journey with bare walls and empty drawers all around me, all the better to enter with the Lord into the ritual reliving of his Passover through death to new life.

After a glorious Easter Vigil service of prayer the night before, on Easter morning the social gathering following the liturgy was filled with "good-bye hugs," leaving me with a readiness to—as the gospel had said that morning—"Go into Galilee and meet the Lord there." I felt that with the Lord by my side leading me on, there was nothing to fear. "So I go forth in confidence, following the directives of your Spirit, that all shall be well, and all shall be well, and all manner of things shall be well."

Chapter 7

WASHINGTON, DC

The drive-down day was huge. Up at 6:00 a.m. closing the final bags, then off to the U-Haul rental place, and back home with the truck by 8:15 a.m. One of my confreres as well as a couple friends were there to assist me, and together we loaded the truck in an hour and three-quarters. I was on the road by 11:00 a.m. with my ten-footer U-Haul packed to the gills.

As I got within an hour or so of DC, the leaves on the trees were starting to open, and with proximity to DC, blossoming trees began to appear. Nature was singing "Christ is risen!" The drive down was bright and sunny and cool, a lovely early spring day.

The following morning, hard to believe, there I was, sitting by the window of my new room, almost completely moved in. Just a few days later, I participated in my first "family-time" session with the priests in the house. It was a great way to "connect" early on, and I was delighted to learn that such an event for substantive sharing took place at regular intervals in the rhythm of their community life. In New York City, I had to initiate it, and it was less frequent (monthly, as this would be biweekly). Marvelous!

I'd been watching my reactions to things as I moved from one place to another, and I made a "litany" of things I liked in my new environment:

THINGS I LIKE

Natural light flooding passageways and rooms
Seeing the blue sky and clouds
Flowering trees right outside the window

Grass and flowers
The relative quiet at night
The worship space
Morning prayer, said more slowly, and with singing
The blessed sacrament chapel: a lovely place to meditate
Conversational ease at round tables in the dining room
Gym in the basement, complete with whirlpool and sauna and a locker room!
A big spacious library with available computers to use
The interaction of students and priests
The cobblestone courtyard with the colorful circle of tulips smack in the middle
The lawn chairs and table under the trees outside on the back terrace

When I got up in the morning and opened the drapes, there was the sky and tree tops! Glory! No shouts from the street, no sirens, no generator noise. Just a natural scene. Halleluia!

AN INVITATION OUT OF THE BLUE

Soon, in 2007, I was on the road again, this time to San Francisco where I did a number of things at our two parishes there: a three-hour workshop with the Old St. Mary's church staff and another for the Holy Family pastoral council and interested parishioners; preached four Masses on the weekend and gave a well-attended talk to the public on Monday evening.

After about a year-and-a-half in Washington, I received an invitation from my confrere Michael McGarry inviting me to consider applying to succeed him in his nine-year directorship at Tantur, an international ecumenical institute for advanced theological research in Jerusalem, on a hill near Bethlehem. When one looks it up online, one reads "an oasis where one can be refreshed in heart, mind, and spirit."

I talked about it with my spiritual director, and responded to his questions, sharing that I felt like I was firing on all cylinders in DC and experiencing the invitations that were coming—more than I could respond to—as the Lord's way of letting me know that I'm right where he wants me to be, and to just "keep on keeping on" and not looking for greener pastures somewhere else.

In the end he confirmed my own instincts/intuitions in the matter, noting that it hadn't been all that long since I moved to DC, and was only now beginning to feel somewhat at home in the seminary community and in the District. Pick up and move again?

"Why would you want to go somewhere in which you don't know anyone and no one knows you, and begin again from square one? With your far-flung engagements here," he said, "it seems that you're able to touch more lives by just remaining where you are. It's taken you a couple of years to develop your network here and establish credibility. The peace you're feeling is a manifestation that you're aware of God's invitation to you and are following it. I would suggest you write back to Mike and say, 'Thank you very much for thinking of me. I'm honored. But my sense here is that I'm right where the Lord wants me to be, doing what I should be doing.'"

And that's what I did, though I'm sure Tantur would have been an enriching experience in its own way. I felt a deep and immense gratitude for this call of the Holy Spirit that I have felt from early on in my theological studies. Way back then, the very word *ecumenism* had a special aura about it. My favorite periodical and the only one I subscribed to after ordination was Ecumenical Trends. After twenty-eight years of full-time work in this field, to realize how it continued to stimulate me and motivate me, to feel the gratitude I felt, was tantamount to an affirmation that I was right where the Lord wanted me to be. And that night, I wrote in my journal: "Thank you, Lord, for the call to serve the unity of your followers. I am at a loss to explain to others how I continue to love this ministry and feel energized by it."

In the weeks following, occasioned by some engagements in my home state of Minnesota, several people asked me how I was feeling about being in DC. It was now at about the year-and-a-half mark for me there, and it felt not only like a good place to be today, but like home.

What made it so? Down-to-earth things. At morning prayer, most people in the house took their presence and participation in the community prayer seriously. I valued that. At the breakfast table, I'd sat down that morning and talked with one fellow from Germany and another from Scotland, both here for the twentieth anniversary of the John Paul II Institute. We had a good conversation, and I learned some new things. At noon, I lunched in our dining room with the Dean of Students at the Washington Theological Union. There was a flow of people through the house that afforded a regular fare of stimulating conversation.

The upshot is that I was feeling very blessed just to be there. My clear sense was that the Spirit truly had been leading the way, from Montreal to New York City and now to DC. The variety of engagements that were popping up all around me there were another expression of it: A day at the Benedictine Pastoral Center in Bristow, Virginia. My upcoming first talk in a seven-month series at the Washington Cathedral. A day for faith formation directors. An interfaith panel in Arlington, Virginia, and an array of offerings at Georgetown University that connected with the ministry I was involved in. In the upcoming week alone I saw that on Monday I would be engaging with Focolare at the John Paul II cultural center; on Tuesday, going to the interfaith concert at the National Cathedral; on Thursday, going to Hans Kung's talk on Christianity, Judaism, and Islam at Georgetown University, with an invitation to a private reception and supper after.

Did I want to go somewhere else? No. The call I felt was just to reap the harvest of the field in front of me. Another of the invitations that had come was to accept a position at the Secretariat for Ecumenical and Interfaith Affairs at the U.S. Conference of Catholic Bishops, which was located right next to St. Paul's College where I lived. While it, too, would have had real benefits, there were several reasons why I was not moved to accept it.

I wanted to be able to have the opportunity for up-close work with the "people on the ground" and not be working in a bureaucratic structure. The main work of the office would be the regional and national dialogues among largely academics or religious "professionals," and beyond that, the ethic would be to "stay in the office." While the theological dialogues are very important in resolving our divisions, I did not see the dialogues reaching the people or changing their lives in any significant way. Further, there was no one to step in for me and carry forward the work I was doing for the Paulist Fathers. Finally, I liked the freedom just to follow the Spirit's movements in my ministry. When I shared my decision with my spiritual director, he spontaneously blurted out, "Oh, that's a good decision!" When I asked him what he saw in it that caused him to respond thus, he said, "The desire to be 'hands-on,' doing things that reach people...

sounds like the inspiration for the Word of God becoming flesh in Jesus, doesn't it? God wanted to be close to us, and wants us to be close to one another."

When I framed for him my present quandary of how to slow down, to recognize the line between giving *of* myself and giving *up* myself, his answer went in the direction of "Let the Lord guide and direct your work." But, I asked, am I to presume "the Lord" is in every invitation that comes, and that he wants me to try to accept all of them?

His response was, "When an invitation comes that feels too tight, what are the priorities that guide you? You need the formal prayer time to help you bring intimate, spontaneous communication with the Lord into the rest of your day. A good examen question would be: What were the places when my work became prayer today? How do you put value on 'the ordinary' of your day? The prep work is not just prep for one particular thing or another, but for all that will fill the day of ministry. At some point the gift *is* your schedule. When it feels too tight, what are your priorities?"

The following day, I "wrote to my body" in a journal entry reflecting on my priorities:

> Dear Body, I know I've been pushing you to the limit of late. It is my firm intention to back off, to ease up on the engagements that require me to spend even the evening hours of the day in the office working, that deprive me at times of a free hour to swim in the pool, exercise in the gym, do my 2nd meditation, or read a book that feeds my spirit. I can do better, and promise to make every effort to do so. Thank you for supporting me with good health. I do not take it for granted and do not wish to abuse it. The best way I can show my appreciation is by balancing work with exercise, soul-food reading, time with friends, and rest. The person I bring to the ministry will be more grounded, energetic, and joyful, and those I seek to serve will reap the benefits of a genuinely holistic spirituality.

The challenges to live this more balanced life and holistic spirituality kept on coming. Within one week, in came five new invitations: To lead a morning for youth ministers in the archdiocese of DC. A weekend at the Dominican House in Virginia. A day at the Benedictine Pastoral Center in Manassas, Maryland. A five-day interfaith retreat at the Kripalu Center in Massachusetts. And an eight-day retreat on the Christian Mystics at Wisdom House in Connecticut.

Life would continue to be both challenging and rich!

VALUABLE PERSPECTIVES

In the summer of 2009, I had the opportunity to lead a week of sessions in Saskatoon, Saskatchewan, where I benefited from a wonderful combination of ecumenical experiences in my Canadian years. It was a week in which the Lord lifted the veil a bit and let me see how some of the seeds we sow do fall on fertile ground and spring up to new life, sixty-, eighty-, and one hundredfold. Nick Jesson, then ecumenical officer for the diocese and past director of the Prairie Centre for Ecumenism founded by Bernard de Margerie, shared how he first heard about ecumenism in a talk I gave in Winnipeg, Manitoba, in 1982, and "the hook went in deep" he said. Margot Taylor also shared around the outdoor table over a beer how the talks I gave in Saskatoon in 1983 had inspired her to work with Bernard in founding the Prairie Centre for Ecumenism the following year. Bernard, at his anniversary dinner the following night, referred to me as his "friend and mentor in these past decades," and then ended his talk with a prayer I had written:

> **REJOICING IN OUR DIFFERENCES**
> When God puts us back together again (with the aid of our willingness to cooperate), this great Church will be marked by the dignity and reverence of the Anglicans, the order and sacraments of the Roman Catholics, the warm fellowship of the United Church, the Presbyterian desire for good preaching, and the Lutheran respect for sound theology. There will be the Baptist concern for individual salvation, the Congregational respect for the rights of lay members, the Pentecostal reliance on the power of the Holy Spirit, and the Quaker appreciation for silence. We will find there the Mennonite sense of community, the social action of the Salvation Army, and the Reformed

> love of the Bible, all wrapped in Orthodox reverence before the mystery of God.

A few years later in 2012, in leading a couple days with thirty campus ministers from around the state of Minnesota at St. John's University in Collegeville, Minnesota, the interchanges with the campus ministers, about half of whom were in mid-life range and half of whom were young adults, gave me valuable perspectives.

One was that I was immersed in my own world of ecumenical and interfaith interchange, reading and reflection, and it wasn't a "bubble" inhabited by many others. Another insight was that young adults of college age who were going to church were in that phase of their human development where they were trying to create an identity. They were much more interested in learning more about Catholicism and its distinctiveness than about other traditions of Christian faith and their commonality with Catholicism. I'd heard that theme at other universities as well. It made me aware that finding ways to interest that constituency in the message I was bringing for Christian unity made it all-the-more challenging.

My approach is that one of the things that marks us as Catholics is our openness to the "other," the Protestant, the Muslim, the immigrant. The Roman Catholic Church's commitment to Christian unity, its openness to world religions, its strong social teaching, all exemplify that openness. It is one of the salient features that distinguishes us as Catholics. As to whether "the ecumenical movement has a future," if it doesn't, it can only mean that we've chosen to ignore a critical dimension of the gospel. It's not about being successful in terms of results; it's about being faithful to the gospel and witnessing to the gift of reconciliation in our lives.

Chapter 8

ON-THE-ROAD MINISTRY: GOSPEL CALL

In the thirty years between 1980 and 2010, tremendous convergence had taken place among churches through the liturgical and biblical renewals and through the ecumenical movement. Teams of theologians working together in national and international dialogues made significant progress in resolving centuries-old church-dividing questions. Through their joint work and prayer, they grew together in faith. I felt, however, that such opportunities now needed to be made available in each place. In other words, church members needed an opportunity to "receive" those gains. My conviction was that the time had come to take advances in Christian unity efforts "to the pews."

One of the historical Paulist ministries is the preaching of parish missions in which a Paulist preaches in four to five evening prayer services in a Catholic parish. Observing that the different denominations seemed so into "branding" and identity-buttressing that nobody seemed to even use the language of church unity, I decided to put an ecumenical spin on the parish mission ministry, naming it Gospel Call, and inviting one of my ecumenical colleagues to be a co-leader and preaching partner with me.

During my years in Canada, my preaching partner for these five-day Ecumenical Parish Missions cosponsored by four-to-six churches was my Anglican friend, Rev. William Derby. We would preach together at a Sunday morning service in each of the churches, as well as at a prayer service that would take place each evening in a different denominational church to which all the other churches would come. The invitations came from across the country: Victoria, British Columbia; Winnipeg, Saskatchewan; Toronto, Ontario, as well as from interesting places in the United States like Washington, DC, and Memphis, Tennessee.

On one of the evenings, dedicated church people from the co-sponsoring congregations would break into discussion groups and share what they did, discovering the commonality of their experiences and what they could do to support each other. Together, they would identify two key goals they wanted to work on, for example, establishing a communications network among themselves, and/or a resource center for all their use. And we would put in place a committee of representatives from all the congregations to carry their project or goals forward. A rich yield—one that could change their relationships significantly for the better and have a positive impact on how they responded to their mission as churches in their area.

This whole mission experience was a raft ride down the Grand Canyon of God's grace, lifting my heart and mind beyond description. A luncheon workshop that we offered on The Ecumenical Gift Exchange drew about a hundred people, consistent with all the other midday events. The topic lent itself to stories with laughter and heads nodding in understanding, and when it came time for the people to engage with one another in their own faith-sharing, the room was popping with energy. A gentleman came up to both William and I afterward and said that he thought it was the best session of them all.

In a mission we co-led in Montreal, there was a very good turnout and in the ritual action of lighting candle tapers from the paschal candle in one of the evening services, the Anglican Archbishop Richard Smith was there and gave a six- to seven-minute introductory talk, thanking William and I for planting the seeds. "This event is your 'baby' grown up," he said.

Our evening homilies felt good to me. Each night it was a deep joy to proclaim the Word, and to do it in a way—team preaching—that kept the people's attention. So many people came up to us at the final evening reception to express their appreciation for the whole mission and the inspiration it had provided them.

This was the prayer within me: "Lord, all I can say is a deep, heartfelt 'Thank you!' for using me in this way, to be your seed sower, a flute to your lips, sandals on your feet to facilitate your reaching minds and touching hearts far and near. I feel so *blessed* to have been given the privilege of serving you in this way."

Prior to the closing evening service, the organizing committee members took William and me out for supper. They all seemed thrilled with the way the week had unfolded. One of the things they said was, "You know, our other mission speakers have all had themes like the scriptures or justice and peace. And what we've really appreciated about this mission is that you and William have consistently addressed the theme of Christian unity." That they would actually express positive appreciation for focusing on a theme that for so many has just fallen off the screen, was music to my ears!

When I moved back to the United States, I invited a Protestant colleague, Rev. Diane Kessler, who served as the director of the Massachusetts Council of Churches, to be my preaching partner and co-leader for Gospel Call. She was a real pro and I enjoyed working with her. We both brought our gifts to the endeavor, and good things happened through this synergy. We preached individually during at least one Sunday service in each of the co-sponsoring congregations. Then we would preach together in jointly sponsored prayer services on Sunday, Monday, and Tuesday evenings. On Wednesday evenings, we would facilitate a sharing among representatives from the sponsoring congregations who participated in similar ministries.

Before the evening service Sunday, there was a potluck supper, jointly sponsored and organized by the participating congregations. On Monday, Tuesday, and Wednesday, following the evening services, everyone was invited to gather in the hosting congregation's fellowship hall for refreshments and socializing. Once during the course of each weekday, a different spiritual growth and development opportunity was offered by the missioners in the form of a breakfast workshop for people on their way to work in the morning, or a midmorning Bible study, or a luncheon reflection. Similarly, these sessions took place in the various churches to provide people with an opportunity to become comfortable entering each other's churches.

On the last evening, Wednesday, people engaged in similar ministries in the various cosponsoring congregations came together, for example, youth ministry; liturgy and music; social action; administration; Christian education. In a session beginning and ending with prayer, Diane and I would lead representatives from the cosponsoring congregations in a process of sharing with one another what they did, the resources they used, and whether they perceived any ways they could support each other's efforts or act together. This provided direction for ongoing collaboration between the local churches as they faced the future. Most of those who came the first night kept coming back for the ensuing three evenings.

One of our Gospel Call Lenten missions was in North Caldwell, New Jersey. I was really struck and touched by the quality of the four pastors involved and the positive relationship that already existed among them, now strengthened by this event.

The Catholic pastor, Fr. Anthony, hosted a breakfast for the planning team and the office staffs of the three congregations. It gave the office staffers an opportunity to meet and create a relationship, and for the planning team it provided an opportunity to underline that they *did* want to see some effective follow-up come out of this. They were going to get together again after Easter and go over the poster-paper sheets of ideas produced by each of the breakout groups that met on Wednesday night following the prayer service.

In short, Gospel Call was really energizing for congregational members who participated. They repeatedly told us how nurtured they were by the services and sermons, and how wonderful it was to be doing this together. There was lots of wonderful synergy on the final day.

Another Gospel Call mission that Diane and I led in Denham Springs, Louisiana, was also co-sponsored by four congregations: Episcopal, Roman Catholic, and two United Methodist, and one of the four was an African American congregation.

On the final night, we put people into five different kinds of ministry groups with ten to fourteen in each group. Good facilitators were selected by the pastors. They came forward with enough ideas to fill the big whiteboard with things they might do better. Diane shared her reflections on the points the planning committee should take into consideration as they looked at the proposals.

Many went out of their way to come up and thank us for coming and leading Gospel Call. Rev. Deborah of the African American congregation told Dan Krutz that she thought it was the best thing that had ever happened in Denham Springs. And Dan himself, a lifetime veteran of the ecumenical movement as executive director of the Louisiana State Council of Churches, told Diane and I that the week had "exceeded my hopes and expectations in every way."

Diane shared that Gospel Call was a living-out of spiritual ecumenism at its best in a substantive event in which the seeds planted have the potential to grow and bear significant fruit into the future. "In an era where the goal of organic unity seems like a dream, where mutual recognition of ministry and sacraments are being hit with new hailstones," she observed, "Gospel Call represents a way of keeping the energy flowing by doing together what it's possible for us to do."

Eventually, however, Diane let me know that, given her responsibilities as Director of the Massachusetts Council of Churches, she couldn't come up with the time and energy needed for both ministries. She also knew that another ecumenical colleague of mine, Rev. John Armstrong, had expressed interest in preaching some Gospel Call missions with me.

A couple of weeks later, I talked for an hour on the phone with my Evangelical friend John in Illinois, a conversation that ended up with our praying together. When I put the phone down, I just sat in silence for several minutes, palpably aware of the Lord's presence. Later that afternoon, John sent an email saying that he had put two upcoming Gospel Call missions, one in Columbus, Ohio, and the other in Montreal, Quebec, in his calendar. "These dates are merely held until we see how the Lord might lead. I look forward to beginning this new ministry with you and believe we could, by the Lord's kindness, be a wonderful team as brothers and dear friends. Yours in his grace, John."

I had a new preaching partner! In our phone conversation, he shared that he had been praying to deepen a relationship with a Catholic who shared his passion for Christian unity, and with whom he could engage in something that would reach people in transformative ways. When, after our phone conversation, we met and talked in Chicago, he took the Gospel Call material home with him. After reading it, he called me to say, "While I was reading it, I said to myself: 'This is what I've been looking for!' How could I not feel your directing hand in this, Lord?"

Chapter 9

RETREATS

Things kept on coming in the retreat ministry as well! I received an email from Maggie McCarty in the Christian Brothers Office inviting me to lead a day of retreat for directors and staff of five non-profit Catholic agencies in Washington, DC. When I called her with an affirmative response and began to discuss with her possible themes, the church's mission for unity is the one that went "click" with her!

As time went on, St. Paul's College hosted a day cosponsored by the Washington Theological Consortium (WTC) and the U.S. Conference of Bishops' Secretariat for Ecumenical and Interfaith Affairs on "Emerging Trends in Ecumenism." It brought together another fifty people from a wide range of denominations. I was working on my talk right up to the last minute. The director of the WTC, Larry Goleman, had invited me to share with people the various ways in which I try to bring the church's mission for unity to the folks in the pews. In writing my talk, I realized that it was an opportunity for me to succinctly summarize the graces of the past twenty-five-plus years: Gospel Call, Unitas, ecumenical retreats, and the newsletter *Koinonia*. When Larry introduced me, he said, "I think of Tom kind of like a John Wesley, touching people's hearts devotionally, or like a Johnny Appleseed, out there sowing seeds of unity here, there, and everywhere." I felt blessed by those associations, and several people expressed their appreciation after my talk and said that it had energized them.

The retreats, offered on ten different themes, generally envisioned people of Christian backgrounds and sought to open them to an experience of how all we hold in common in Christ is much broader and deeper than what still divides us. In the retreat setting, people are away from their customary preoccupations, their hearts and minds are open, they rest and relax, and new possibilities emerge. It is through sharing such time, space, and experience that people change their perceptions of one another and form new relationships. Some of the retreat themes were also sufficiently universal to include both Christians and members of other world religions in a shared retreat experience.

RETREAT THEMES

Together in Christ: Themes for reflection are the biblical call to unity among the followers of Jesus, what we hold in common, learning from our differences, the importance of respect and trust, the role of the personal in ecumenical relations, contributions each of us can make to Christian unity, qualities needed for the journey, and gifts to be received from other traditions of Christian faith as well as from other world religions.

Cultivating a Holistic Spirituality: Daily morning and afternoon conferences focus on components of a holistic spirituality: Exercise and Play, Time with Friends, Recovering a Weekly Sabbath, Prayerful Presence in Daily Living, Service, Work, Creation and Creativity, Time Alone and in Community, Various Ways of Praying, and the Role of the Body in Prayer.

Prayer of Heart and Body: An introduction to meditative prayer in the Christian tradition and to the role of the body in prayer. A devotional approach to meditation and to yoga postures linked in graceful, flowing movements to song-prayers is taught as a way of anchoring one's practice in the soil of Christian faith and praying through the full expression of one's being.

Remember to Live: Awareness and acceptance of second-half-of-life realities like aging and health challenges can bring clarity and richness to the limited, precious moments of life, and foster a special care for relationships and priorities. This retreat offers a faith-filled way of facing our finitude, of preparing for and integrating loss, whether of things or loved ones, all the while awakening us on a deeper level to the gift of life that is ours to live *now*.

Pray All Ways: Contemplative living keeps our antennae up and receiver station open to the messages always coming from the Sender. Participants will learn and practice fresh approaches to meditation, to praying with the scriptures, with beads, with intercessions, with the daily examination of consciousness, with the body, to living with an awakened heart and to praying in all circumstances.

Taking Your Prayer to a Deeper Level: We will both open up the treasure chest of the history and theology of Christian contemplative prayer and engage in its practice through a recovered manner of praying with the scriptures known as *lectio divina*, as well as a morning and late-afternoon quiet sitting in Christian meditation/centering prayer.

Becoming Free: Based on archetypal themes in the *Spiritual Exercises* of Ignatius of Loyola, the daily program includes presentations on four steps to spiritual freedom—Know who you are; Live your calling to the full; Let go of results; Daily rededicate your life to God—as well as time for personal reflection and inner work. The focus is not just on freedom *from* but on freedom *for* commitment and the inner liberty it brings.

Lessons from the Mystics: The treasure trove of Christian mystical writings testifies that the mystic is one who is consciously immersed in the experience of God's closeness and love in daily living. We will explore major themes in the tradition and cross-reference characteristics of the mystics lives with our own.

Soul Fire: Accessing Your Creativity: The creative potential within us is one of the things that make us "in the image and likeness of God." The focus is on helping you identify your creative energy, overcome your insecurities, and connect with your chosen method of expression. The Creator has gifted you with creativity; your gift in return is to use it.

Inspiration Near and Far: We're increasingly living in religiously plural communities. Is our response one of suspicion and fear, or one of dialogue and mutual enrichment? We will reflect on Catholic perspectives of other religions; learn about the various forms of dialogue; deepen our appreciation for what we share; and identify areas of mutual challenge and inspiration for our living. Through it all, we will see how one of the fruits of the interfaith encounter is often a deeper appreciation for what is distinctive about our own faith.

One of the reasons that I loved the retreat ministry was that each retreat required me to re-engage with practices of the spiritual life that are conduits of grace. In preparing for the talks, I had to read through the content again. In giving the talk, I wanted to speak about this practice with conviction and out of personal experience. That implied a recommitment to it on my part. Any practice can become "rote" or "occasional" for us rather than mindful and regular or frequent. So leading the retreat and giving the talks reenergized these practices in my own life and renewed my commitment to them.

Leading the retreats in various places also gave me the opportunity to see friends there once again and to enjoy some quality time together. A wonderful example of such: After leading a retreat in 2019 at Queenswood on Vancouver Island in British Columbia I was able to enjoy with a friend some wonderful walks on the beaches of the Pacific Rim National Park in BC. And then, after another retreat at the FCJ Centre in Calgary, Alberta, was able to take with long-time friends in Calgary some magnificent hikes in the Rockies on Bustall Pass one day and Yamnuska the next, followed by the opportunity to see my godson Brendan's premier showing of "The Y Generation" at a Calgary theatre.

From there it was on to Arizona to give three talks to church leaders there on their annual retreat day. The talks stimulated good sharing among themselves. In their feedback at the end, they said they felt the day had strengthened their relationships with one another and their commitment to ecumenism. The United Methodist Church leader came up to me, put her hands on my shoulders, and said, "It's not easy to lead a day for church leaders and get into their hearts and minds and move them, but you did that with us today."

A couple notes slipped under my door said, "Thank you for allowing God to use you in your vocation for us. As a priest, as a retreat master, as a writer, as a spiritual director and confessor, and as a friend."

"Thank you for being faithful on your spiritual journey and allowing God to 'touch' you with Divine Energy of Love. May you continue to gift others with the message of how *real* God is and wants to be in our lives."

In a weekend retreat at the Providence Centre in Edmonton, Alberta, the group of twenty-five retreatants included Lutherans, Mennonites, Orthodox, and Catholics. I felt so blessed to be able to engage with life-giving themes of prayer, meditation, and a holistic incarnational spirituality as part of my ministry. At the very end, the program director asked me to stand in the center and lead everyone in singing a blessing over me. As they departed, there was a prayer that arose within me: "I feel so privileged to be a flute to your lips, Lord, bringing people the music that brightens their lives."

Chapter 10

THE MOVE TO BOSTON

In 2015–16, the financial burden of keeping our large seminary building—St. Paul's College in Washington, DC—up and going in its current state led to a significant decision to put this historic site of ours up for sale. We had rented space in the building to eighteen different national offices, all of whom would also now have to find a new "home." What with all the closings and sales of religious houses in the area, it was becoming more and more difficult to find available space for rent. It was painful for us all as the personnel in these different offices not only had found the space in our building in which to do their work for the church but shared their ministerial experience and built community with many others in the various offices. It had been a "win-win" both for them and for us Paulists who needed the revenue to pay for the upkeep of this huge building, but who also appreciated the contact with these other church workers. The Hecker Center wing of St. Paul's College was going to be a ghost town in the year to come, a new lay-of-the-land that would occasion another move for me. But where?

In concelebrating at the National Shrine in DC on the Feast of the Ascension, I was struck by the question posed by the preacher in his homily: "Did you ever have an experience of 'Where do I go from here?'" He proceeded to talk about the inner feeling of uncertainty and wonderment that must have inhabited the disciples after Jesus's "goodbye" and departure/ascension. Then he ended with the words "God will not abandon you. God will send the Holy Spirit to lead and guide you on the way forward." I took those words with me, and when I was taking a prayerful walk around the side altars behind the main altar, the inscription beneath the big mosaic of Christ spoke to me: "I will send the Advocate. I will prepare a place for you."

Psalm 16 in the day's scripture reading really spoke to me as well:

> Keep me O God, for in you I take refuge...it is you who hold fast my lot.
> I bless the Lord who counsels me; even in the night my heart exhorts me;
> With you at my right hand I shall not be disturbed.
> Therefore my heart is glad and my soul rejoices; my body too abides in confidence;
> Because you will not abandon my soul to the nether world,
> Nor will you suffer your faithful one to undergo corruption.
> But you will show me the path to life, fullness of joys in your presence,
> The delights at your right hand forever.

The gospel reading that day was "spot on" as well—John 17:20–26, reaffirming me in my work for the unity of Jesus's followers. The prayer that rose up within me: "I thank you, Lord, for the encouragement and reassurance given me by your Word this day. All shall be well, and all shall be well, and all manner of things shall be well."

Shortly afterward, a little box from Paulist Press was in front of my mailbox, containing a few copies of my new book *Christian Unity: How You Can Make a Difference*. I took it up to the Blessed Sacrament chapel and knelt down, putting the box on the kneeler next to me, taking out a book and then just holding it in my hands as my offering—yes, a sacrifice—to the Lord. Forty years of ministry, Lord, symbolized in this little offering. Then I just knelt there for some time, soaking in the moment with gratitude that the book would make possible a new sowing of this seed hither and yon and that it would hopefully take root and grow in myriad hearts in ways unimaginable.

What would be my new home for the work of the Paulist Office for Ecumenical and Interfaith Relations (POEIR), a move required by the changes taking place among the Paulist community in DC? After exploring various possibilities, I opted for another East Coast city: Boston.

The Paulist Center is located in the heart of downtown Boston, and just about anything one might want to go to—a pharmacy, barbershop, restaurant, clothing store, movie theatre, fitness center—is a short walk three to five minutes from our door. The residential architecture in the neighborhood is historical with cobblestone streets and sidewalks lining the stone-and-brick constructed homes.

The Paulist Center residence, offices, meeting rooms, and chapel are also just a half-block down from the golden-domed State House, right across the street from the beautiful half-mile long adjacent city parks of Boston Common and Gardens, at the end of which is a pedestrian bridge over to the Esplanade, a walkway and bike trail along the Charles River. All-in-all, hard to beat!

One of the things that drew me to the city ministerially were two networks, one ecumenical (UniteBoston) and one interreligious (Cooperative Metropolitan Ministries). It wasn't long before I was serving on the Board of Directors for each of them. The range and activeness of their ministries are inspiring models for similar networks in cities around the country. I continued to participate in the Catholic-Hindu national dialogue as well as the Catholic-Muslim regional dialogue.

Shortly after my move in the spring of 2016 I got a call from Bob Flanagan in Illinois, the Director of the Catholic Association of Diocesan Ecumenical and Interreligious Officers (CADEIO). "Tom, I've called you to let you know that you're the recipient of the Fitzgerald Award this year, given for outstanding contribution to the work for Christian unity and interreligious understanding."

When I put the phone down, I felt suddenly washed over by a big wave of blessing and just looked at the painting on my wall of Jesus. "You did it, Lord, and your timing could hardly be better... the year in which I did my best to harvest the fruit of decades of working for the unity of your followers in my new book...the season of my departure from DC and all the colleagues and friends there. I receive this as a sign of your love and appreciation, and I am deeply touched by your kindness. I am happy to be on that list of recipients with two other Paulists, Tom Stransky and Ron Roberson, both of whom have also given their ministerial lives to serving the unity of your followers."

In January 2017, my first Week of Prayer for Christian Unity in Boston exemplified the richness of ecumenical networks in the city. One evening I went to a prayer service at St. Mary Antiochian Orthodox Church in which there was a prayer service with Coptic Orthodox co-leadership. On another evening I participated in a prayer service at Lion of Judah Pentecostal Church. And on the Saturday of the week there was a marvelous four-hour event at the Roman Catholic Holy Family Church in a suburb. It began with lunch, followed by a forty-minute workshop that I led on "What Gifts Do We Have to Offer to One Another?" followed by an extraordinary Prayer Service for Christian Unity in which clergy from twenty-two different churches all processed in, robed, to the chant of a Coptic Orthodox choir. It was co-presided by the Catholic cardinal archbishop, the Eastern Orthodox archbishop, and a representative of the African American Alliance. Cardinal O'Malley preached a very solid homily for Christian unity, followed by intercessory prayers, Orthodox chants, and candle lighting. The processional and recessional lines were like microcosms of the universal church in terms of denominations, ethnicity, color, and liturgical attire. It was truly inspiring! It was one of the richest Weeks of Prayer for Christian Unity I had experienced in all my years of full-time ecumenical ministry.

With so many indicators over these past years of less and less wind in the sails of the good ship Ecumenism, it was very heartening to come to a city where ecumenical networks like UniteBoston and the Ecumenical Institute are succeeding in billowing the sails. I was grateful to the Holy Spirit for leading me here when I was facing the difficult decision of where to move POEIR to after seven years in New York City and nine in Washington, DC. In neither of those cities was there as lively networks as the ones I was discovering—and becoming part of—in Boston. It pumped up my tires for my remaining years of service and would help me finish strong.

In the fall of 2021, after forty-five years of ecumenical and interfaith ministry in North America, I handed off the baton to my Paulist confrere Fr. James Diluzio in New York City to carry forward the work of the Paulist Office for Ecumenical and Interfaith Relations.

Part Three

SPIRITUALITY

Chapter 11

OUTWARD BOUND

What makes a ministerial autobiography like this possible? I would have to say journal keeping. I began this practice with the conviction that each day is special and carries something of significance in it. A journal would help me catch the significance of each day. Making an entry later never succeeds in conveying freshly the feelings that were current at that moment. Entries made days later tend to be analytical, detached, "from a distance," which they already are. So I have dedicated myself over the years to making a brief entry nightly, and to try to break the pattern that creeps in from time to time of writing only at "significant times." I began this practice in the conviction that each day was special and carried something of significance in it, and a journal would help me catch the significance of each day's living. That conviction has helped me maintain the practice.

In 1972, after my first year in the Paulist seminary, I engaged in a two-week-long summer Outward Bound wilderness survival program in northern Minnesota, the "Land of Lakes." A lover of the outdoors, I was eager but mindful of the challenges ahead that were likely going to cost a lot physically, emotionally, and mentally. Toward the end of the experience, each of us would be left behind and alone on an island for the final three of the fourteen days, called a "solo."

When it rained, it was sometimes all day—while we paddled, while we pitched our tents, while we ate, while we did the dishes. When you're out in the wilds, the weather is really the home you live in and adjust to. There's no getting away from it. When you have no alternative but to meet the weather on its own terms, you tend to look at it differently.

For instance, I had never liked rain as far back as I can remember. When it rains, my tendency is to get indoors away from it because rain makes you wet, makes you uncomfortable, and gives you colds. But this was a different experience of rain for me. You can only get so wet, and when you resign yourself to that and reach that point of saturation, you find out it isn't so bad. In fact, it even feels neat on your face when it falls, and it's like the sky is making all these happy little doodle circles on the big sketch board of the lake.

What drew me to the Outward Bound experience? Well, it struck me as a form of "spiritual exercises" aimed at emptying out the areas of one's life where there has been too much growth, for example, self-centeredness, and doing some growing in areas such as awareness and concern for others. Theology talks about "kenosis," that is, emptying oneself in order to be filled. A tough double-portage is a very real form of *kenosis*. Once you've crossed over and want to just take off your pack and lie down and rest, you also feel yourself called to just remove your pack and head back to help another, overcoming the inclination to self-gratification in favor of the good of others.

Anytime one learns to give more and count the cost less, there is fuller humanness present. One experiences oneself functioning best as a human being when one's focus is outward in service. Any program that can further that movement is making a real contribution to individuals and to the human community, which can only realize itself through the service orientation of its members. I found it appropriate that the first words of the Outward Bound motto are "to serve."

When it came time for our solo experience on an island, each of us was allowed to bring only what we could wear (all of us were down to carrying just the essentials on this fourteen-day trip, so there wasn't a lot to choose from). I wore about everything I had: a T-shirt, turtleneck, wool shirt; two pairs of socks, two pairs of pants (one wet, one dry), and my rain gear. And apart from clothing, I had five matches, three fishhooks, a solo tarp, forty feet of fishing line, and my little journal and a pen. Outward Bound's food policy with regard to the three day "solo" is to give the person enough for one meal a day. My food package contained one packet of beef barley soup mix; one packet of mushroom soup mix; a little plastic bag of granola of about two to three inches, and the same of rice. That would be my food for three days.

I found a nice natural shelter in a grove of five trees and strung my solo tarp up over my head, using my shoelaces as tie-strings. When it started to rain in the early evening, I just lay under my tarp watching the rain. It had been a hard day and the rest felt good. Already, however, the mosquitos were swarming. When dark came, I tried to sleep, but I couldn't get used to the idea of just lying there and letting the mosquitos feast on me. How those little devils cut through two pairs of pants I'll never know, but they do! The worst part is their buzzing in the ears. I tied the hood of my rain jacket around my head, and then took my bandana and put it over my face, tucking it in the hood so that my face was fully covered, and put my extra pair of socks over my hands. After that, it was mainly just putting up with the buzzing.

The next day I savored everything in a cup of warm soup. A little "want" goes a long way in terms of appreciation. A meal, even when alone, is a central act. Jesus selected the perfect moment—sitting down gratefully to food—as the "Last Supper" act, which he wished to be commemorative of our appreciating him. Is there anything else to which we so consistently bring feelings of gratitude than to a meal? From there, it is only a short transitional step to see more meaning in the act of eating: it is life-sustaining. The sign of food participates in the reality it signifies (life-giving-ness) and is a sign of greater realities. I trusted the small "want" I would experience in these days would render me more sensitive to the peoples of the world for whom food is approached all the more gratefully because they have so little of it. Every day is a "solo experience" for them.

One of the things I appreciated most in this solo experience was the knowledge that nobody was going to come looking for me, asking me where I'd been or what I was thinking about/doing.

There's a strong strain of independence in me and a great need to be reflective about what's happening in my life and where it's going. I certainly like and enjoy people, but also can appreciate being alone. That's one of the practical reasons that celibacy "works" for me: it affords much interaction with people on a meaningful level, and yet gives me the opportunity to be alone and reflective. I felt quite comfortable with this "solo" experience. It occasioned my discovering more and more the rhythm and sense of rightness that accompanies a simple and uncomplicated mode of existence. I felt close to the earth, good friends with the fire, and a peaceful kinship with solitude.

That is one of the main reasons I could gladly take the promise of poverty again at the seminary at the end of the summer. It's a real help to me in keeping my life simple and preventing me from becoming possessed by a superfluity of material things. There are things more important to me than material goods: a community of people for whom I care and who care for me; the opportunity to serve people and share meaningful life with them; a way of life that is conducive to staying attuned to the movements of a God in my life whom I experience to be gracious and loving and personal.

This experience in the wilderness prompted me to reaffirm my desire for the priesthood because it had been an *experience* in the elements I value and strive to implement more fully into my life: simplicity, prayerfulness, community, service, a close in-touchness with nature, myself, and other people. It seemed to me that a life of ministry best afforded me the opportunity to give myself over to the full pursuit of these things.

Chapter 12

ANNUAL RETREAT: LAKE GEORGE

The Paulists have a couple of islands in the middle of Lake George in upstate New York. On one of them, Hecker Island, named after our founder, the New Yorker Isaac Hecker, there is a small chapel. On the other, Hewit Island, named after Augustine Hewit, one of the formators of the Paulists and the community's second Superior General, there is a cabin.

Coming to these islands eighteen miles down the thirty-two-mile-long lake is often more like a pilgrimage than a vacation retreat. I feel like a pilgrim going to Mecca, and once arrived, incredulous that such good fortune should come to me. If anything, the place becomes more sacred to me with each sojourn there. On arriving, I may bow to the forested mountains on both sides of the lake, kneel and touch my forehead to the ground, then stand up and do an embodied prayer to the Trinity. It is a religious experience for me to come to our Paulist islands, for in my history of annual retreats there, this is the place where my desire for God burns hottest, brightest, and purest.

It usually takes me the first few days to unwind if I've been running a long gauntlet of deadlines in the previous weeks. But once on the island I can release and relax. For example, one year I'd spent the previous month in intensive day-by-day preparations for leading a retreat in Newfoundland, Canada; a Christian Spirituality Conference in Wichita, Kansas; followed by leading two more retreats, one on Facing Mortality and the other a Prayer of Heart and Body retreat. The time between the sessions was generally filled with a one-on-one sharing with the retreatants.

All of this provided the context for why I was feeling such a strong desire for a solitary space in coming to Lake George. When my mind has been literally awash the previous weeks with preoccupations relating to the sessions I would be leading, coming to the island is always an opportunity to let all that go and touch the divine presence within in focused stillness. It is wonderful to have quiet solitude, some good spiritual books and food, the water to swim in and the mountains to look at. It is for me an effective way of recharging depleted batteries. When my retreat on the island is just days away, my inner spirit is standing on tiptoes!

Contemplative awareness would find unique expressions on the island. I might:

Study a spider's gossamer web on the dock.
Play my harmonica while swinging in the hammock.
Notice a seam in the sky where deep blue became azure under the changing angle of light.
Float in the lake, watching a hawk ride the air currents above while he watched me ride the water current below, each envious of the other.
Paddle around to the beaver lodges to note their expansion since last summer.
Dive in the lake after sunset, awed by the silhouette of mountains and the rosy band of color on the horizon.
Sit with eyes closed, listening to the crickets and feeling at home on the planet.

This is the kind of retreat I most desire: peace and beauty, silence and solitude. Reading, prayer, and reflection are what most nourish and rejuvenate me. When I awake in the morning, having slept in the screened-in porch, it's like awakening in paradise to the light, the beauty, the serenity!

After lying in bed and just breathing in the grace and gift of the morning, I usually slip into the water of the lake about 7:30 a.m.—a time at which the whole lake is often without a ripple—and I swim around the island using mostly side, back, and breast strokes because it's too exceedingly beautiful above to put one's head down in the water in the crawl stroke. Once back in the cabin, I'll just spend some time in prayer, resting in God's presence in meditation.

The exhilarating thing about being there is not just the beauty and the serenity, but having a whole day of time in front of you to just do what you want to do. Nobody is coming in the door or over the phone with a request or a deadline that's going to make you revise your plans for the day. One's inner spirit becomes like the early-morning lake, very peaceful, serene, quiet.

MORNING MAGIC

I woke this morning
to the summoning sound
of an immense stillness
which held all creation bound.

The deepening blue
of the pre-dawn light
shhh'd the crickets' mantra
of the night.

Even the woodthrush
had not yet begun to sing
the approaching, glorious advent
of El Sol, the golden king.

I quietly left my bed
—for better or for worse?—
stepping softly to the shore,
afraid to wake the universe.

Asleep before me lay the lake,
held in mountain's firm embrace;
the breeze, too, lay quietly in the wings,
not daring to mar lady water's face.

The mist hung in the valleys,
caressing the forests,
awaiting a sign from the sun
to bring all creation into chorus.

And while all looked away, awaiting another,
—tell no one of this!—
I woke the world myself
diving into the lake, full of bliss!

Time on the island is an exhilarating experience for me. I simply sit for hours under a pine tree on the point in front of the cabin, focusing first on one sense, then another. The breeze playing around the surface of my skin and on the back of my neck, the pine-scented air, the song and chatter of birds, the waves lapping the rocks, the dazzling dome of sunlight on water, and the wondrous beauty all up and down the lake. I just sit there and *look* at things—flies, ants, ferns, bark, and scrub brush—in centered, still, focused awareness. I may get up a couple of times and dive in the water just for the pleasure of its coolness, floating with a life-preserver, looking up at the sky and the trees and the clouds. What a carnival of sensory experience! It may even be a fast day, but even at 5:00 p.m. I feel energized, refreshed, and not the least bit hungry. What a wonderful, quality day with which to enter into my weeklong retreat.

In my annual week's retreat, a good deal of time is devoted to reading and reflecting on the gospels and apostolic letters in the Bible. I feel a call to live the gospel much more radically than I do. I feel a call to go and preach—not a watered-down version of Jesus's teachings, Lord, but the real thing. The assurance rises within that if we *live* the gospel, things will happen. We must deepen our faith and make of our lives a clearer sign that there is something special motivating us.

Is there anything in our lives that we can point to which is explainable by nothing else other than our faith and or trust in God? When there is something that genuinely smells of the gospel, people will cross an ocean to find it. If we live this, people will come from far and wide to get in on it. In Mark's gospel we hear that "Jesus's relatives came to take charge of him because they thought he was crazy." Maybe that's our problem. We're not crazy-enough in the eyes of the world. We're too much like everybody else, and nothing stands out clearly that says "There's something special going on here." People just want to touch somebody who truly believes.

When the apostle Paul speaks of favoring celibacy over marriage, for example, he's not merely speaking of simplifying lifestyle to give more time to ministry. He is speaking of a life that has gone beyond contingent realities and lives in "undivided devotion to the Lord."

To be sure, marriage signals Christ's covenant of love. Singleness makes another, different sign of God's love, a sign that says, ultimately, "God is our satisfaction." Marriage trains us in the service of love. Singleness frees us to see God as the primary source of our love. Both are modes of salvation. Celibacy, as the church fathers practiced it, said, "God is enough." God's love filled their lives and they were, in Paul's words, "devoted to God in both body and spirit" (1 Cor 7:34). What do we find in Christ? At least this:

- healing from past wounds
- forgiveness for past sins
- an example of sacrificial, covenant love
- a purpose that lifts me above my narrow preoccupations
- joy and peace, which radiate the presence of the Holy Spirit
- patience to persevere in difficulties
- strength to control my impulses

KENOSIS AND FREEDOM

In my early years at the Canadian Centre for Ecumenism, a pattern I was seeing is how self-centered life can become. I've always got a full agenda of things I want to read and write, and when somebody comes—whether on the phone, or in the office to see me, or to the house—my inclination is to give them the minimal time that I can without being inhospitable or rude, and then get back to my agenda. I didn't like what I saw there. There was something in this "new job" that could find me getting very insular, and, to my unsettlement, liking it. I saw an energy pattern that I would have to counteract with conscious decisions to interact, to receive that phone call or unexpected visitor within the context of the spirituality of availability.

One year while on retreat, I spent some time reflecting on *kenosis*, that is, self-emptying. The spirituality of kenosis helps us to see how much "control" is a touchstone of our lives. There are so many patterns in my life that seem characterized by control, for example, my approach to time, schedule. Yes, busy people have to do this to accomplish their many tasks, but we spend so much time at the altar of structured control, and so little at the altar of freedom and spontaneity. We are constantly trying to control one situation after another by discipline, by communication, by sheer force of will. The constant temptation is to make our lives secure, closed systems in order to satisfy the desire for control. And when we do not manage to do so, our tendency is often to be impatient and frustrated and self-recriminating with regard to our lapses.

If we could hear God speak, what we would likely hear is "I keep this in your life to try to bring you around to recognize your utter insufficiency. Until you live from self-emptying (kenosis), you do not live by grace." We need to recognize that God is our only hope. Grace inserts itself in our weakness. When I am brought to a point where my own strength fails and where I simply do not seem to have what it takes to do what I would do, it can be a moment of grace. A moment in which God's power is able to step forth and renew me.

Each day and each week brings many occasions for practicing letting-go-of-control, and openness to unforeseen possibilities. I recall, for example, an occasion in which one of my relatives and her daughters asked me to join them for a movie. Which one? I asked, wondering whether it would be one I was interested in seeing or one I wasn't. When it turned out to be the latter, I resisted the temptation to manipulate my choice and went with their preference. And it was a delightful film, a light touch that brought laughter and was surely better for what I needed than the heavy three-hour one that would have been my choice.

Scheduling ourselves in so tightly day after day is a way of preventing the entry of new, unforeseen possibilities. If I want to practice being empty of my own desires and open to new possibilities, I need to (1) allow more room for the unplanned and (2) be ready to drop plans and push schedules aside to respond to the unexpected. This, for me, represents a daily asceticism/spiritual practice. Being out of control, whether it's a question of what movie we see or what gets done on my desk any given day is a reminder that grace is my only hope. Living out of my weaknesses, or my inability to accomplish this or that, is to live by grace.

The strange and wonderful thing is that this being emptied out of my own designs, while seeming to limit my freedom to do what

I want to do, is nothing less than an invitation to enter into the full liberty of spirit—the liberty we enjoy when we are turned away from self. In this way alone lies the continuous expansion of heart, mind, and spirit, growing in love and becoming more firmly rooted in God. My hope is to increasingly live this way with a real sense of enthusiasm and the fun of life flowing from that liberty. So the two words that God seems to have given me over the years are:

1. *Kenosis*: inviting me to a willingness to be emptied out, to discover that my strength is in my weakness, and so to truly rejoice in it because it brings me to where my strength fails and where the only hope is grace.

2. *Freedom*: salvation from my enemies (foremost among them my own controlling tendencies), being brought into an open space of ever-widening perspective and possibilities.

WORK AND THE SPIRITUAL LIFE

In his book *Gratefulness, the Heart of Prayer*, Br. David Steindl-Rast says,

> Working leisurely is no contradiction at all. In fact, work ought to be done with leisure, if it is to be done well.... Should I not also have a good time while I'm working? People who spend their working hours with no mind for anything but purpose are unlikely to begin playing when their free time finally comes. Either they will collapse and slump in a chair...for that kind of work wears one out completely. Or they will be so set in the groove of mere purpose that they will continue to work. Unable to play, they will either work overtime, or if they pick up their golf clubs or tennis racquets, they will give themselves a *work*out. We are simply unable to play playfully unless we learn to work playfully.

Efficiency and productivity are the base of our Western civilization. There is often a constant stream of deadlines or engagements with no room to breathe and simply take a day off. What I realized more and more was that my ecumenical ministry was more and more what I *do*, but the spiritual life was more and more where my passion and energy are. My “job” becomes the workshop of the spiritual life for me in the real world of interpersonal relationships, financial concerns, personnel crises, and so on. These two foci—my work and my spiritual life—have for a long time been twin passions, and the domain of ecumenical work has gotten the lion’s share of attention.

Frankly, it’s not immediately apparent what we might do that would enable us to invest more time and energy to the interior life in a focused way. The main thing is simply to remain calm and open. The Lord will unfold whatever he has in mind for us in his own typically marvelous and unforeseeable way. Each year when we enter into Holy Week and approach Easter, the insight that has been most significant for me is that the Lord’s dying and rising is one mystery. This passing-over is not just an ultimate event; it is not only future but also present. It is an immediate reality, a daily choice. Holy Week plays essentially a consciousness-raising role, helping us to bring to more conscious awareness the pervasive presence of the paschal mystery in our lives throughout the year. “Letting go/dying” does lead to new life.

Chapter 13

FOUND A CENTER FOR SPIRITUALITY?

After working for fourteen years at the Canadian Centre for Ecumenism, I began to feel the Spirit preparing me for a next evolutionary step. My growing interest in spirituality and the increased number of invitations I had received to do work in that area (without soliciting them) were signals to me that in this direction lay my future.

Then, in the pilgrimage I led to India (more on this in part 4), the two inner movements of the Spirit clearly indicated what this Center could be like. That said, the overarching experience in India confirmed for me that ecumenism and interfaith is the context in which this work should be pursued. My taste for learning about and sharing with people interested in the spiritual life and an experience of loving intimacy with God had become so pronounced that I felt sure the Spirit was leading me into this.

As the months rolled forward, two things came to me regarding the Center for Spirituality project: (1) It must maintain its focus on the contemplative and resist being a "catch-all." (2) I must not cling to what is pleasant (e.g., the Ecumenical Center with its good staff and relative financial security) nor react with aversion to the prospect of sacrifice (e.g., moving from an intimate living space where I have my own life, to a large place with more people where private space and a personal life is harder to come by). I could only ask the Lord to help me cling to nothing, void myself of all attachments, and keep myself free and open to doing whatever seems to be his will (kenosis). "Jesus, your one goal was to do the will of our Father, everywhere and in all things."

Once we had moved into the Unitas mansion, the prayer that surfaced was: "Thank you, Lord, for my calling. I love serving you with all my life, by means of these multiple ministries I'm engaged in. Life is particularly joyful right now in a quiet sort of way, interiorly. There is a serene joy and peace."

This was the ministry that over time I longed for, and I was seeing more and more clearly that the Lord was bringing me to it. The invitations to lead retreats and days of prayer had been coming with more and more frequency, and I saw his guiding hand in it all. Were we ready to turn this wonderful mansion in the middle of the city into an ecumenical center for spirituality? All I could say was, "I'm ready to serve...."

Until you commit, things don't begin to happen. It's only after you cross the line and throw in your lot decisively that things do start to jell and fall in place. Trust, trust, trust. Everything needed will be given.

As time went forward, I saw that I was inching perceptively closer to the edge of a new undertaking that would involve the next several years of my life. I knew I could stay where I was as director of the CCE. It was comfortable and secure financially and I had a good team of ten colleagues, but I had felt something moving in the background for the last few years, like the gathering of forces for a new initiative. "Is this it, Lord? Lead me and guide me. Give me the assurance that this is what you want me to do."

As the weeks rolled by, I tried to just let the thoughts, feelings, and fantasies arise without editing them, just observing them. The fantasies were all in the direction of being there, *living* there, and seeing different things happening. Living the laity-clergy partnership. Seeing the dream-inspiration that came to me in India of an ecumenical center for spirituality where people could come and learn the practical disciplines for the Christian life. Seeing a vibrant contemplative community made up of women and men, laity and clergy, at the heart of the city. All the feelings that were coming up were positive. There *is* a monk in me. I've always known it. Was this where I would be able to live it out?

I HAVE A DREAM

Sitting in reflection on a Poustinia Day, the dream within me flowed up and found expression:

I have a dream of a place at the heart of the city where people who are frazzled and stressed can find peace and inner resources.

I have a dream of a place where those who have experienced the "sugar high" of consumer candy and who now hunger for substantive food can come and be richly filled.

I have a dream of a place where those who know God and want to give themselves more totally can find direction and counsel.

I have a dream of a place where the "ways to God" discovered by the different religions can be competently and responsibly opened-up to people who are on a quest and seek to encounter the Holy One.

I have a dream of a place where the richness and beauty of the mystery of Christ can be revealed through the insights and devotions and pieties of all the traditions of Christian faith.

I have a dream of a contemplative Christian community at the heart of the city, made up of women and men, laity and clergy, French and English from several churches, working and worshipping together, serving one another and those who come, living as a parable of reconciliation and a prophetic sign to their churches of the unity to which they are called.

I have a dream of a community of people who drink deeply and regularly from the wellspring of the indwelling Trinity at the core of their being, and who are carried out by the energies of the encounter on a river of service to the needy, the poor, and the downtrodden.

I have a dream of a place where people can go and find the treasure chest of spiritual wisdom thrown open wide and concretely taught.

Is this the place, Lord? It could be. It stands here on the mountain in all the grandeur of its rooms and all the gentle imitation of its arbored garden, awaiting a vision worthy of it.

Am I ready to place my resources, my energy, and the next decade of my life in the service of this vision, this dream? I have worked in campus ministry for six years, and the Canadian Centre for Ecumenism for thirteen. It feels as though it's time to take up a new challenge, to feel new energy in the face of a new beginning.

As Goethe wrote,

> Until one is committed, there is hesitancy, the chance to draw back, always ineffectiveness concerning all acts of initiative and creation. There is one elementary truth the ignorance of which kills countless ideas and splendid plans: That the moment one definitely commits oneself, then Providence moves, too. All sorts of things occur to help one that would otherwise never have occurred. A whole stream of events issue from the decision, raising in one's favor all manner of unforeseen incidents, meetings, and material assistance that no one could have dreamed would come his way. Whatever you can do, or dream you can, begin it. Boldness has genius, power, and magic in it. Begin it now.

UNITAS: THE DREAM IS UNDERWAY

Could we just take it as a three-year run at a noble project and simply enjoy the place, the people, the challenge, but carry it all with a sense of light-hearted detachment? Could we simply give it our "best shot," and if we fail, then we leave? We will have had a few years living in a unique place, doing things we believe in, sharing faith, deepening our prayer. If what happens to us in the process is what we most deeply want, then the whole experience will have been eminently worthwhile.

What do I want? To live my life with greater surrender and faith in God's guidance and care. To learn to serve without counting the cost. To have more time to read and pray. To be able to lead retreats and sessions that flow out of my own passion for God and the spiritual life. To be able to focus my energies and encounters with people on things that really matter to me. Why don't I just do it as an experiment in faith? Just give myself to it and see what it has to teach me?

Could I have been led all this way only to go back now? It was hard for me to accept that, because I really did feel the Holy Spirit had brought me to this point. So my sense was: Why don't I just throw caution, security, and control to the winds and just give myself to it like a fool for Christ? Why don't I just do it as an experiment in faith? Why don't I just give myself to it and see what it has to teach me? Why don't I just come across with an uncharacteristically wild act of abandon? Why don't I enter into this adventure of living with real freedom of spirit that marks those who truly rely on God as their sufficiency? Why don't I just "go for it" and leave plenty of room for the God of surprises?

The secret of the spiritual life is to recognize and consciously accept our oneness with our infinite, eternal, and immortal Source, and to abide in that Presence every single day. And when we formally pray, to remember that we are speaking to a God who is already within us, not one we have to go off and seek. Therefore we can pray at the office or while doing housework, whether walking, driving a car, or riding a metro. We can literally pray without ceasing because there is always room in our consciousness for a remembrance, a realization of God within us.

As our programs at Unitas took root and began to grow, I realized more and more that I was relating to people on the level of my heart's desire, to talk with people about God, about the interior life. This is the vibratory level I want to lock in on with people. The opportunity was increasingly there for it. As my spiritual director said to me: "Be faithful to what burns deepest and brightest in you. Don't sell out on that just to make somebody else happy." My feeling was that as long as I can continue to do this ministry, I'll go anywhere. It's the relating and sharing in this vibratory zone that feeds and energizes me.

Chapter 14

NEW DEVELOPMENTS

It was a few years later that Frank Desiano, the president of the Paulists, began communicating with me regarding his desire to create a ministry and office that expresses the component in the Paulist Mission Direction Statement relating to Christian unity. If allowed to integrate the retreat ministry into that and use any available time between the two for writing, well, that could be attractive. In any case, I saw the handwriting on the wall: within a couple more years I would likely be back in the United States to make myself more available to help the community move its ecumenical agenda to higher ground.

Two years later, in 1999, came the shock of the Unitas Board of Directors announcing that it was looking for a new building and pledging money from the sale of the Unitas mansion in support of programming and staff salaries. I went to the chapel and sat, remembering the afternoon five years earlier when, following the ecumenical prayer service blessing the house and the project, I had gone to the chapel feeling a wave of energy like a sailor setting out on a sail across the sea, rejoicing that we had actually left shore and were setting off on this adventurous journey.

A week later, my friend Jim sent this message:

> Been wanting to let you know I've been thinking of you and all the troops at Unitas and praying for you. As I've reflected on the beauty and power of Unitas, it was not that "magical museum" you were housed in that was so special and memorable. Rather it was the community that lived, worked, served, learned, worshipped, and

loved there. The community of Jesus that incarnated the essence of the Unitas program and God's love right there. That's what I will miss the most. What drew me most to Unitas and all that went on there was the context: a real Christian community of God's wonderful people. And the good thing is that it can continue there in Montreal and elsewhere if people continue to be called to it.

FAREWELL AND TRANSITION

After life and ministry in Montreal for twenty-two years, my departure was as graceful as I had hoped it would be. With the unexpected developments at Unitas, it seemed the right time for me to go. I wasn't grieving, looking back. The present and future were so rich and full of promise that my eyes and heart were turned forward. To be sure, the leaving was not without pathos (tears at the final Eucharist together), but it was smooth because of the year-long period of anticipation and preparation and my own readiness in the end to "just do it." And it would be made doable by an upcoming three-month sabbatical.

My immediate destination, the Paulist summer place at Lake George in upstate New York, made it all the easier. The first few days at the main house were given to socializing with my confreres, indulgence in the wonderful meals, and in the water games of sailing and water skiing. But after a few days there, my soul began to yearn for the solitude and the natural beauty of Hewitt Island.

Always on arriving there I am stunned that I could be delivered to this pristine place with healthy food, all this natural beauty, and no phones, email, fax machines, visitors at the door. I spent a couple weeks of peace and quiet there as an entry into my upcoming sabbatical time of two to three weeks for writing, followed by a forty-day retreat elsewhere. In all, about two and a half months of quiet with no other responsibility than to listen and allow myself to be guided by the inner movement of the indwelling Spirit. In short, to prepare for the next step in my ministerial journey.

Reading and reflecting and writing are constitutive elements in my rejuvenating process. The rest of the year I would be following schedules and very likely a chock-a-block agenda of engagements, but in my island time followed by sabbatical time, all that would be "out of the picture," leaving me free to follow the inner urgings of the Holy Spirit from rising to sleeping.

I remembered the time in my college years when Mom and Dad were selling their large home for a smaller, simpler place to live. Mom just walked into the living room one morning and said to my sister and I as she looked out over the snow, "This is beautiful. We won't have it next year...but I just felt the call of God to live more humbly and simply. We spend so much of our time and energy taking care of worldly things. I just want to get closer to God!" And her eyes teared up. When she left, I said to my sister, Mary Jane, "Let there be no doubt as to where we get our desire for God." She replied, "We get our spiritual desires genetically, just like we inherit physical features."

As I entered into my sabbatical time, my spiritual director's counsel to me was, "Stay close to your desire for God, your inner fire, and it will govern you discretely in all your living." That inner fire—the enabling power of God—sustains us. Discovering that we can rely on this inner strength from above establishes an inner authority, a freedom from within out of which we can live even when the outer supports are not there. This was a capital lesson the Holy Spirit wanted to teach me.

Part Four

DAILY SPIRITUAL PRACTICES

Spiritual practices were planted in me early on in my life as both my mother and father were deeply spiritual people whose faith found expression in various ways throughout each day. They would make their way to the local parish for early morning daily Mass. At home, Mom would sit in a prayer corner she created in the house and pray with beads before a statue of Mary, while Dad would pray the psalms for the day from a monthly prayer book. During Advent and Lent, before going to bed, we would gather as a family for night prayer.

Loyola catholic high school that I went to took each class to a retreat center for an annual week-long retreat. In my senior year, while on retreat and kneeling in front of a statue of Jesus in the chapel, I felt the Lord speaking to me and calling me to become a priest.

When the time came for graduation, though I had received an academic and athletic scholarship to St. John's University in Collegeville, Minnesota, where as an all-state running back I would love to have played on the Johnnies football team, I decided to enter the seminary.

Chapter 15

THE EUCHARIST AND PERSONAL FORMS OF PRAYER

As previously mentioned, my parents' daily participation in the Eucharist planted the seeds in me for a better understanding of the nature and content of this form of prayer. Understanding the context of the Last Supper is essential to comprehend what Jesus was instituting. The Last Supper was a Passover meal where Jews remember the Exodus and thank God for his gracious acts toward his people. Here they also renew their covenant with God.

The Eucharist is therefore to be seen as a sacrificial meal where we give thanks to God, especially for the gift of his son; where we renew the new covenant with him; and where we are united with him through Christ. The very word *Eucharist* means "thanksgiving." In the Eucharistic Prayer said by the priest at Mass, we pray to the Father through, with, and in Christ. We give thanks and praise to God for his wondrous deeds, especially for raising up Jesus as our savior. The Eucharistic Prayer asks that the Spirit transform us so that we can become like Christ, or as St. Augustine said, that "we become what we receive." Ultimately, one might say, the Mass is more about *us* becoming the body of Christ than it is about the *bread* becoming the body of Christ.

The Mass renews the covenant that commits us to follow in Christ's footsteps in loving our brothers and sisters, especially the poor and the marginalized. The Eucharist is about making us more

Christlike so that we can continue his mission of establishing the kingdom of God, of bringing justice and peace to the world.[1]

Jesus is the Word of God who came down from heaven, was born of the Virgin Mary through the power of the Holy Spirit, and became a human person in a specific time and place, Bethlehem and Nazareth. But each day when we celebrate the Eucharist, Jesus comes down again from heaven, takes bread and wine, and by the power of the Holy Spirit becomes our food and drink. In short, God's incarnation continues to happen at any time and at any place. Jesus is closer to us now than he was to his own apostles. Today, he is our daily bread!

That was literally the case in the lives of both my dad and mom. They went to Mass every day. On the weekdays it would be the early morning Eucharist after which my dad would be off to a full day's work at Ryan Grain and Feed Elevator and my mom back home to care for five kids. On Sundays, we would all go together to the mid-morning "family Mass." We lived just a block away from the parish church.

The seed they planted in me through their own spiritual practice took root and grew in my life as well. Listening to the Word of God in the daily scripture readings and receiving holy communion has continued to be at the core of each day's living for me. In the combined liturgy of Word and Eucharist, receiving divine wisdom and nourishment each day is at the core of my spiritual life.

PERSONAL FORMS OF PRAYER

There are, of course, many forms of prayer, and one could say that it is not even we who pray, but Christ who prays in us. We do not pray; *we are prayed*. We should, each of us, discover what is the form of prayer to which God calls us, integrating that into a certain regular amount of other forms of prayer and worship. Then we will have a truly balanced spiritual life. In his book *Paths to Personal Prayer*, Evan Pilkington provides some concrete examples of what "quick prayer" might sound like: In moments of

> Thankfulness and joy: "Thanks be to God!"
> Anxiety: "Father into your hands I commend my spirit..."
> Fear: "Lord, hold me. Lord, save me."

Doubt and indecision: "Lord, guide me."
Weakness and temptation: "Lord, strengthen me."
Sin: "Lord, have mercy."

Before anything we do, especially if we are scared about saying and doing the right thing (e.g., before taking a call, writing an email, going to talk to someone), we can offer a quick prayer: "Lord, use me." After we've offered it, however things appear to have gone, a quick "Thank you, Lord, for using me."

One might say that there are two forms of prayer: (1) occupational prayer: directing our thoughts to God in all our activities; (2) spousal prayer: dealing with God directly and immediately. The greatest index of whether we love someone is how much time we spend together. The reason why early in the day is best for some quality time together is that our energy is best when it's fresh. The Spirit will teach us how to pray. What we must do is dispose ourselves. This is the heart of the discipline of prayer: to take the time. To go to your quiet place. To dispose yourself.

A massage experience can be a wonderful analogy for disposing oneself for an encounter with God. You undress, sit in a steam room to get the circulation flowing, and finally lay down on the massage table, supple and ready and relaxed for the massage. That's what the disciplines of Christian living do: they prepare us, dispose us to be acted upon by the Spirit of God, whose probing, expert touch heals, unbinds, restores, and releases new vitality for fuller living. Afterward, one feels more rooted, centered, peaceful.

In the following chapters, we will take a closer look at several of those personal forms of prayer.

Chapter 16

CHRISTIAN MEDITATION

In 1975, I was ordained in the Paulist Fathers, and my first assignment was to the Ohio State University Newman Center in Columbus, Ohio. As I look back, I see the Spirit working in my life and gradually leading me to a meditative form of prayer. During my college years, my spiritual director was integrating a method for it into his own prayer life as a religious, and talking with him and learning more about it was a beginning for me.

In 1977, when I was sent to direct the McGill University Newman Centre in Montreal, Quebec, I was happy to learn that the Benedictine John Main, the eventual founder of the World Community for Christian Meditation (WCCM) now located in Bonnevaux, France, had come that very year with his confrere Laurence Freeman to found and develop a Christian Meditation Centre in Montreal, just a few blocks away from the Newman Centre. When I heard about the prayer form he taught, I sought him out and he subsequently became my spiritual director. His teaching and practice guided and inspired me. He died on December 30, 1982, but the words of advice that he gave me were continual compass bearings for me. The core of his counsel was, "Continue to say your mantra. Stay on pilgrimage. Persevere."

Today, the WCCM is a global spiritual community united in the practice of meditation in the Christian tradition. Its members now span more than a hundred countries, and its international center is Bonnevaux, an ancient monastic site near Poitiers in France, now dedicated to global peace and dialogue. In the spirit of serving the unity of all, community members gather daily for meditation as passed on through the teaching of John Main and his successor Laurence Freeman.

What helped me to integrate time for meditation into my daily rhythm was a subsequent deeply spiritual experience I once had in the middle of the night. I experienced the Holy Spirit giving me a mantra to pray with and to share with others. What I heard was, "Jesus is in you. Breathe in the love of the Father for the Son as you pray his name: *Je-sus*. Then breathe out the love of the Son for the Father as you pray: *Ab-ba*. As the love that passes between the Father and the Son is the Holy Spirit, as you breathe-in again, pray *Ho-ly*, and as you breathe-out, *Spir-it*. Pray with this mantra throughout the time of meditation, synchronizing it with your breathing, simply resting in Trinitarian love."

As anyone who has ever sought to practice mantra meditation knows, it is indeed challenging to anchor the mind. The practice of meditation could be characterized as having some similarity to what happens to us when we sit down to our computer. We normally have a particular site in mind, but when various notices pop up on the screen, we end up "surfing the internet," randomly visiting "various sites" with our mind becoming a veritable web-browser. When we realize we're not focusing on what we had originally intended, we give a little "click" to our "mental mouse," that is, returning to our mantra. The effect is like when the screen saver is on and one clicks the mouse. The program that we originally logged into, and which had faded out due to lack of attention, unfurls once again on the "screen" of our mind.

In order to hold it there, however, we have to keep working in that program. Once our attention shifts and we open another window on screen or stop what we're doing to take a telephone call, we lose the site and have to click on it once again. The "click of the will" that refocuses us on God's presence and reasserts our intention is like a little click of the mouse. Keeping the screen of our consciousness on the desired program requires constant, patient "clicking."

I'd have to say that meditation is an important cornerstone in my spiritual life. It has no agenda. It just calls for focus on the gracious mystery of God's love present to me, and just being in and soaking in it. And yes, one must be very firm and uncompromising in the face of temptations to give up one or the other time of meditation on any given day. It's repeatedly a question of priorities.

As for the practice of meditation, in our utilitarian culture where we suffer from a collective compulsion to do something practical, helpful, or useful, and where we feel compelled to do something that can give us a sense of worth, contemplative prayer may feel sometimes like a waste of time because it's not useful or practical. That said, it cuts a hole in our busyness and reminds us why we were created: to enter into a relationship of love with our Creator and to deepen it until we ultimately enter into eternal union with the one who is love itself. Prayer is this experience of relationship, of communion, of oneness with that experience of God's love.

Chapter 17

SPIRITUAL READING

There are so many books out there that are rich in spiritual content. One just has to begin and be led by what one reads and finds inspiring and helpful. For me, John of the Cross came to the top of my list. I found so many levels of resonance with his writing that he became my official patron. He was a writer and a poet, an energetic worker with several balls in the air all at the same time. In his various roles of definitor and provincial and consultor he was constantly traveling—way before it was *a la mode*, on foot and by donkey, staying in rundown inns, traveling light, living simply. He had strong women friends in his life like Teresa of Avila and Ana de Jesus. He had a special bond with his mother. Of course, he was a contemplative and a mystic. His spirituality was markedly trinitarian, with Jesus in highest profile.

His four major works and their commentaries became major sources of inspiration for me. *God Speaks in the Night*,[1] a book on his life, times, and teaching, was the centerpiece of one of my retreats, and has made a profound and lasting impression on me. And it came as a delight and "wink" from God to read on the last page of it: "Fr. Isaac Hecker, founder of the Paulists, was an avid reader of the mystical Doctor, choosing him as patron of his 'active community.'"

Some of the lines that spoke to me from John of the Cross: "We have little hope for union with God when there is no quiet in our lives. We need to cultivate an interior secret space, away from the daily commotion, so that we can hear the voice of love constantly addressing us" (p. 129), but he was a contemplative in action and did not live in undisturbed solitude. The highest state of union for John is spiritual marriage, which is a total transformation into the

Beloved. It is a surrender of the entire self to the other in love. In John's words, "My personal relationship with God is meant to reach completion in spiritual union, and in doing so, shares the life of the Trinity. Our entire lives are meant for one thing only: to share divine life."

Of course, the scriptures are a daily source of nourishment for our journey. Two things strike me in the fourteenth chapter of Luke's gospel in which the daughter of Herodias demands the head of John the Baptist. How fast John's life ended! How long had he been sitting there in prison? Then suddenly "the girl *hurried* back with her request: Give me *at once* on a platter the head." Then the king promptly dispatched the executioner who went off and beheaded him in prison. John the Baptist was probably just sitting there, and suddenly there are footsteps, the gate is opened, in walks the executioner with a sword and a command to John to position himself thus, and swoosh! It's over!

A second thing that strikes me is the suffering, violent, painful end of so many of those to whom God has given a special calling. John, Jesus, Peter, Paul, and *all the disciples*. It's scary, but it's also a powerful indication that God's ways are not our ways and that suffering is a valued instrument in God's toolbox. This is another thing that impresses me about John of the Cross: he had this remarkable esteem for suffering, and even after his nine months in prison with no light and almost nothing to eat in a small cell, when he gets out and visits the nuns in a local monastery and they start singing to him of how God gives good things to those who suffer, he begins to weep and motions to them to stop, saying that he fears he "has not suffered enough to merit the good things of God."

Would you say we have a lot to learn? The prospect of suffering causes us to recoil in fear. That said, it also gives us a clearer sense of the grace to ask for: Make me, Lord, a great lover—of you, of my brothers in community, of my family members and friends, of those you give me to serve on retreats and missions, of your creation. Make me more generous, ready to go the extra mile, to let go of my own schedule and plans when another's needs present themselves. Teach me, Lord, how to love. Make me a faithful and generous brother, uncle, godfather, and friend, with phone calls and gifts of presence and thoughtfulness.

Expand my heart, Lord. When the verses of the spiritual canticle pass through my mind, it is clear to me how love became the driving force of everything in the life of John of the Cross ("now that my every act is love"). This touches me profoundly and encapsulates my deepest aspiration: to let God's love become the driving force of my life, day after day, and spiritual reading helps provide me with the nourishment needed for the journey.

Chapter 18

PRAYER WITH BEADS

As I mentioned earlier, praying with beads was another daily prayer practice for my mother, and once a week the whole family would gather in a prayer circle and pray the Rosary together. It was another form of prayer that eventually took root in my own life in my college years when I was away from home. I came to appreciate how beaded prayer is the contemplation of the events of God's story with us in creation and redemption. For example, when we are reflecting on the events of Jesus's life, we can apply his battles to the battles in our own lives. I came to experience it not as a flight from the world of daily challenges, but as an embrace of the risen Lord amid our struggles.

One of the things that I particularly like about this form of prayer is that I can pray it anywhere—while sitting in a chair in my room, while taking a walk in the park, while driving a car, while standing in a line at the bank or grocery store, while folding laundry. It's like a portable chapel that we can keep in our pocket and pull out at any time and in any place, and begin reflecting on the mysteries of Christ's life. The invitation is to ponder the key moments in his life—his birth, public ministry, death, and resurrection—and in these mysteries to find the meaning of our own life's story: from joy to sorrow, from suffering to triumph.

In short, the Rosary—from the Latin word *rosarium*, which means "wreath of roses"—is meant to be a prayer that leads us to Christ and into a deepening communion with God. Just as each Hail Mary prayer builds up to the word *Jesus*, so the entire Rosary is designed to lead to union with him. Through Jesus, we come into union with the triune God. Thus, each decade ends with "Glory be to the Father, and to the Son, and to the Holy Spirit," indicating that the whole Rosary is a movement toward praise and joyful union with God. As Pope John Paul II emphasized in the apostolic letter *Rosarium Virginis Mariae*, "One thing is clear: although the repeated Hail Mary is addressed directly to Mary, it is to Jesus that the act of love is ultimately directed, with and through her" (no. 26).

My interfaith ministry gave me opportunities to see that using prayer beads is as old as human history. Christians are not the only ones who pray with beads—Hindus, Buddhists, and Muslims also pray with beads. What is it about beaded prayer that is helpful and that would occasion such prayer among the religions of the world? The beads help the mind to focus. The use of repetition as a tool for contemplation is an ancient practice. Repeating a sacred phrase or verses from the scriptures in rhythm with one's breathing is a method of contemplative prayer in various religious traditions. Hindus, for example, use mantras—the repeating of sacred words—as an aid to contemplation. Eastern Christians use the Jesus Prayer ("Lord Jesus Christ, Son of God, have mercy on me, a sinner"). It's a method that also finds expression in Christian meditation/centering prayer. Just as the repetition of prayer words can lead to a contemplative state, so also can the soothing repetition of touch.

I've found it to be true that beads are one of many tools to assist us in prayer, which is often a struggle because our minds wander, we get bored, we're not sure what to say. Prayer beads have been helpful for me in developing a sense of closeness with God. They're helpful not just to count the repetitions in prayer, but to help ground and center one's attention in meditation, as well as to relieve tension, worry, and stress. In short, my experience has been that praying with beads has spiritual, physical, emotional, and psychological effects. It releases the stress of daily problems, concerns, and apprehensions. Beads can become an appreciable tool in prayer. Just holding them in our fingers is a way of understanding that God is as close to us as the beads in our hand.[1]

Chapter 19

WEEKLY FASTING

I first learned about fasting when I was in the second grade and preparing for my first holy communion. In those days, when one was going to receive holy communion at Mass, one was not to eat or drink anything from midnight the night before. My religion teacher at school said that not eating or drinking was to help build up our anticipation of meeting Jesus. On Fridays throughout the year, everyone seven years of age and older abstained from meat. Plus, on all the weekdays during Lent, those between twenty-one and sixty-five years of age could have only one full meal a day. My parents said we abstained from meat on Fridays as a little reminder of how much Jesus loved us in giving his life for us on the cross. It was our way of saying that we were sorry for our sins and that we wanted to show our appreciation for being forgiven by doing something out of love for him.

In 1966, after the Second Vatican Council, Pope Paul VI revamped the existing discipline in his apostolic constitution on fasting and abstinence (*Poenitemini*). The new rules changed the age at which Catholics should begin to observe abstinence from seven to fourteen years and changed the age at which they ceased to be obliged to their sixtieth year. More significantly, Pope Paul VI authorized bishops' conferences to adapt the directives to suit modern conditions and to emphasize prayer and works of charity as substitutes for previous practices of abstinence and fasting. I was in my second year of college when these changes were announced. The leadership was summoning us to be adults in the faith, to act responsibly and with awareness. Whereas the Roman Catholic Church used to stress both the need-for and the how-to details of this spiritual practice of fasting, it was now choosing just to reaffirm the need-for and leave the details up to its members.

My first assignment after ordination in 1975 was to the Catholic Student Center at the Ohio State University in Columbus. A Day of Fast for World Hunger, sponsored by the university campus ministry, provided me with a new experience in fasting. It was the first time that I had ever gone a whole day without food. There was a prayer vigil that evening at which people gave the money that they would have spent on food that day. Half of it went to a neighborhood soup kitchen for the homeless, and the other half went to the organization Bread for the World. Something in the experience touched my heart and left me with intimations of a power in fasting that I wanted to explore further.

In doing so, I saw that there were two approaches to benefits of the practice: physical and spiritual. The directives from the health-food store gave you the body-ecology approach and the resources from the church the spirituality approach. What I did not find were books or articles that helped people to integrate the physical *and* the spiritual benefits of fasting. It doesn't have to be either/or, I told myself. It can and should be both, because we are not just bodies and we are not just spirits. We are embodied spirits and "enspirited flesh." Confining a means of spiritual growth to the six weeks of Lent made no sense either. Either it was potentially supportive for Christian *life* throughout the year, or it could be dispensed without great loss in Lent. I strove to take a holistic approach, one dealing with the human person as an embodied spirit. As I did so, I saw it, on the one hand, as an action that renews contact with God and, on the other hand, as an action that removed the clutter and excess that could be removed from my body with benefit. The body accumulates a lot of mucus and toxins and chemicals that, if unloaded, enable the vital current of life to flow through us much more freely. If your digestive system is weighed down, overloaded, lethargic, that's going to influence your heart response to God concerning your experience of the goodness of life. But if you feel that everything is running smoothly, if you feel the energy flowing, if you feel calm and peaceful with yourself, productive and useful to others—in short, healthy—then how much more easily prayer will come!

I began reintroducing the practice into my life on a weekly basis, from after supper on Thursday up to supper on Friday, advancing the spiritual dimension of the day by praying, reading the scriptures, writing in my journal or taking a rosary-walk in a local park during the time normally set aside for eating. Spirituality today is asking us to pray from where we are, that is to say, to live with God-consciousness. To lift up our hearts and minds to God in all our circumstances. God is not simply "out there," but in your body and spirit, in your neighbor, in your efforts to work for a just society, in your struggles and joy, in your eating and fasting.[1]

In every age the church must interpret the old truths in new, fresh forms. The climate of spirituality in our age is incarnational. Practices are embraced because of their liberating, life-giving potential, rather than being aimed at punishing the body or compensating for guilt. It is the goodness of creation that is emphasized, rather than the transitory quality of life or the pervasive presence of sin. A healthy contemporary Christian asceticism will not attack or deny what has already been redeemed.

Here are twelve characteristics that have marked, for me, a rediscovery of fasting as a valuable spiritual life practice among Christians today:

1. *It is freely embraced out of a personally perceived value.* The point at which our human freedom reaches its peak is when we, having experienced in our daily lives the abundant love of God for us, move freely and spontaneously to return God's love.
2. *Its two "wings" are prayer and almsgiving.* This approach deepens one's relationship with the Lord and strengthens the community.
3. *It is sensitive to and follows the Spirit's lead.* This prevents it from becoming a technique taken on solely for health purposes or expanded consciousness.
4. *It is not just for Lent but for the entire Christian life.* If prayer, fasting, and works of charity and justice form the core of Christian life and are inextricably linked, how can any one of them be quarantined to just one season of the liturgical year? They are all essential elements of Christian living throughout the year.
5. *It accords priority to that day in the week when Jesus revealed God's immeasurable love for us: Friday.* A valuable point of reference is the pattern in the early Christian centuries: fasting was generally understood as abstinence from

food until evening, or one meal a day, which was to be as simple as possible.

6. *It finds meaningful expression in preparation for receiving the Eucharist.* Forgoing whatever meal precedes Sunday worship creates a psychic as well as physical space within. When something or someone greater is coming our way, we are generally willing to put the eating on hold.
7. *Its approach is holistic.* I am not body and soul (two things); I am enspirited flesh, one reality. What is good for my soul is good for my body and vice versa.
8. *Its characteristic virtue is humility.* We are created from nothing, and God wants us to recognize that we are always utterly dependent on our Creator for all good things.
9. *It is marked by moderation.* Like everything else in the spiritual life, it is not about doing it all or doing it right; it is just about doing it in a spirit of faith and love.
10. *It often has traces of quiet joy within it.* It is only when fasting is experienced as a "body language" of spiritual communication (mystical union) with the risen one and longing for future fulfilment that we can understand why it is characterized by quiet joy.
11. *It stays close to its mystical inspiration.* For so many, Christianity is a moral matter, whereas, in fact, it is a mystical matter. "Mystical" here refers to our participation in the very life of God by our being "in Christ." When we get the relationship part right, the moral living follows naturally.
12. *It is a flexible instrument of the spiritual life that can be used creatively.* Unity in the Holy Spirit, together with great diversity, has characterized the life of the church in its healthiest eras. The choice is between a variety of realizations, united in spirit, and conformity without spirit, which is a sin against and extinguishes the Holy Spirit.

In every culture and religion in history, fasting has been an instinctive and essential language in human communication with God. Let us not be the ones who forget the reasons, the rituals, and the words.[2]

Chapter 20

DAILY EXAMEN

Another helpful spiritual practice is the daily examen, a practice derived from the *Spiritual Exercises* of Ignatius of Loyola, a sixteenth-century Spanish priest and founder of the Society of Jesus (Jesuits). In working with the examen, one reviews the day, looking at things we need for our spiritual growth, and asking the Lord from one period of our lives to another if this is what he wants us to prioritize now. So, when I review my day in the examen, I look to see whether time and energy was given to the Eucharist, meditation, the scriptures, spiritual reading from a book or journal that nourishes my soul, prayer with beads, time with friends.

As I'm now in the process of entering into what the Paulist community calls "Senior Ministry Status" (retirement, SMS), I'm happy to say that there is less stress regarding productivity. Given my good health and energy, however, I decided to just "trim the sails" rather than anchoring the boat. I, fortunately, did have a successor to whom I could hand off the national events and quarterly newsletter but did want to stay engaged locally and regionally. And yes, crossing the line into SMS in that manner still leaves me sometimes experiencing SMS as "So Much Stuff" rather than Senior Ministry Status. Mornings are devoted to snail mail and reading the prep docs for upcoming dialogues like the regional Muslim-Catholic dialogue or tuning into online seminars and workshops. The afternoons and/or evenings can be filled with reading through the hundred emails of the day.

Another topic for my examen focus is daily quiet time—for prayer, reading, and reflection. If I had more time with my own inner thoughts, I could more easily give attention to others. One of my friends sent me an inspiring email that left me with a holy envy for the steps he was taking in his life to scale back on productivity and increase time for reflection and meditation. His life sounded so sane, balanced, *healthy*.

My inner response to it was, "Wow. I *want that*!" This would involve rebuttressing my Sabbath and Poustinia days, my afternoon meditation time, my morning reading time, and my evenings. If I had more such time, presumably my mind would not be so backlogged.

While the last two years of the pandemic have significantly reduced travel, talks, retreats, conferences, and meetings, the "Zoom" era has simply transferred many of the in-person events to online events, with the result that there are now sometimes even more meetings and dialogues than would be the case were travel required.

To keep my spiritual practices in place, I take the time each evening before going to bed to reflect on the events of the day in my journal, and at the end of each week to write in the calendar in my room the name of the friend with whom some quality time was enjoyed. The reason for all of this? "Spirituality is a growing intimacy with God experienced through the people, places, events, and things of everyday life."

Part Five

FINDING A BETTER BALANCE IN LIVING

Chapter 21

SLOWING DOWN AND CENTERING

In my years at Unitas (1994–99), my aspirations were to find a calmer, more centered lifestyle and work schedule. But it was challenging, as I continued to be on-the-road leading retreats. For example, as I was sitting in the Vancouver airport in British Columbia, Canada, waiting for a flight connection to Kamloops, British Columbia, to lead a retreat for Anglicans, Catholics, and Lutherans, I realized I was tired. The night before, I had worked until 12:45 a.m. just pulling talks together. When you add travel, it's not only the preparation for your engagements that puts you "in the hole," but all the things that will accumulate while you're away and be awaiting attention upon your return. It was the same thing I experienced at the Canadian Centre for Ecumenism. Had I just moved this pattern to a new location (Unitas)? What happened to my vision and resolve that my "new life" would be more leisurely, with more time for reading, reflection, and talking with people?

Even at Unitas there were several things happening that I didn't like, for example, spending from 8:30 a.m. to 10:00 p.m. in the office, not finding enough time for spiritual reading, and taking a few days away for refreshment from intensive stretches of work time. When returning did not succeed in doing so with a restored balance between work time and personal time, I quickly burned through the fresh energy by going right back into the pattern of working morning, noon, and night. The lesson I most needed to learn was, "Less is more!"

I needed to tend more to the space between events. I had no right to complain to anyone about it because I myself had said yes, one by one, to all the events on my too-tight schedule. The challenge was to live it in as relaxed a manner as possible so that the lack of time between events would be offset by my manner of living each event. The overall goal however was to reclaim personal space and time for reading, journaling, writing, being with my thoughts, noticing people and things. In short, savoring life!

Have you ever engaged with the Life Wheel exercise? Available online, the Wheel usually consists of eight to ten categories/spokes on the wheel, each one considered an important domain for a whole or balanced life, for example, Family, Significant Other, Personal Growth, Friends and Leisure, Home Environment, Career, Money, Health, and Fun and Recreation. You rate your level of satisfaction with each area, then map this onto an image of a wheel that gives you an overview of your current "life balance." The Wheel helps one to become more self-aware and more motivated to make changes and create a fulfilling life.

In the Life Wheel exercise, the two spokes generally needing attention for me are Fun and Recreation, and Friends and Leisure. The rest, happily, are strong. So my own aspiration has been to combine the two in arranging on a monthly basis to get out and do something entertaining and enlivening with a friend. To relax more, laugh more—at myself and life. To be less intense. To bring more balance into my life, and to take more time with people, to give them priority over things/projects.

As we headed into Winter planning at Unitas, I resolved to (1) do less and (2) leave larger spaces between what I do so as to prepare calmly and without undue pressure. My prayer was, "Slow me down, Lord, I want to enjoy living in this beautiful place and connecting with the people who come here. I want to have more time for and with them." One of the reasons I wanted to step out of my job at the CCE and go to Unitas was to be less busy and have more time for people.

When, after twenty-two years in Canada, the Paulist leadership called me back to the Unites States to open a Paulist national office for Ecumenical and Interfaith Relations at our mother church in New York City, the rhythm of life changed once again. Soon I was participating in regional and national dialogues, leading ecumenical and interfaith retreats, and preaching ecumenical missions with a Protestant preaching partner on themes that touch life's core meaning. I was also rooted in a vibrant parish community with an opportunity to preach and celebrate the Eucharist and get to know people. If I'd been told I had just one year yet to live, my only response would have been "Thank you, it's great!"

I THANK YOU, GOD

I thank you, God
  for music
  and the warmth of the hearth,
  for walking trails in the woods
  covered with a carpet of autumn leaves.

I thank you for hot, homemade soup,
  bread fresh from the oven,
  and the cold, refreshing water of running streams;
  for the gratuity of the stars at night
  and the sky's color at dawn and dusk.

I thank you for the smile that melts the cold heart,
  the laughter that dissolves tension
  the comfort of a friend's presence,
  for our bodies that tremble and
  surge with energy at a gentle hug.

I thank you for so many years of life,
so many people met,
so many lives shared,
so many telephone calls and letters,
so many soft snowfalls and summer evenings.

I thank you, God.
If the curtain fell now,
it would fall on a player in full bow,
grateful for the part entrusted to him
and for the message he was given to speak.

There was still, however, something I wanted to improve about my life: pace, for example, time to get into the rhythm of the community's life, read some periodicals, go for walks with confreres, get caught up with stuff that accumulates in the office during my absence, and to explore the city more. The recurring question: Do I need to limit my time away to a certain number of weeks each year? It's difficult to impose something like "allow two weeks between engagements" because a wonderful invitation arrives, one that *should* be accepted, and it's back-to-back with one already in my calendar, which often looked something like this:

- three talks to Lutheran, Anglican, Roman Catholic clergy in Phoenix, Arizona
- three talks to church leaders in Chicago
- four talks to clergy and laity in Chicago
- overnight with Paulists at Old St. Mary's parish in Chicago
- three days back home in New York City to teach a Prayer of Heart and Body class; to overnight and help out at the shelter for the homeless; to catch up with office accumulation; and to begin packing for the next trip....

LISTENING

We spend 80 percent of our waking hours communicating: speaking, listening, writing, and reading. Some studies have indicated however that in about 75 percent of that time we're not fully present. The average attention span for an adult is said to be about fifteen seconds.

The art of listening is to become "a listening presence." It's a way of being that opens us up so that we can listen to people of different backgrounds and cultures. It's about being open, curious.

How can I impact a situation by the way that I listen? There's value in taking time to practice listening. Listening, one might say, is an art. Like the art of coaching or teaching. When someone is really engaged with an art, they are at one with it. It makes people feel connected, understood, whole, refreshed. Listening as an art is more of a way of "being" than just something we "do."

Listening is a choice. If we really do listen, it may change our minds about something, and we may not be ready for that to happen. Listening is not passive; it's an action. It takes energy. We have to choose to do it.

Listening is also a gift and listening to one another with total attention is one of the greatest gifts we can give to one another. Not only are we present to each other but also to something beyond ourselves. It's "being in the zone." Time stands still. As Martin Buber once said, "When two people relate to each other authentically, God is an electricity that surges between them."

Listening is half of all communication. It's an art and we have a choice to engage in the gift of it. If we want to excel at something, we have to *practice it*. Here are three practices in that regard:

1. Cultivating silence: there's no listening without silence. We need to stop doing, to be quiet, to learn to listen to the silence. Begin the practice with just a minute a day and gradually expand it. Notice what you hear. Give it your full attention.
2. Reflection: slow down to reflect. Listen to your true self. Before speaking, ask if these words are true? Necessary? Kind? What wants to be said next? When someone stops speaking, pause for a moment, then ask them if there's anything else they'd like to say.
3. Becoming present: listening from the heart. For a minute or two each day, be fully aware of what you're doing. *Continuous partial attention* has become our way of being. We have to train our concentration so as to be

able to be in the present moment, that is, to practice mindfulness.

Slowing down, centering, listening are ongoing challenges, but one of the spiritual practices that can really help us to do so is keeping the weekly Sabbath day.

Chapter 22

LIVING WITH A SABBATH RHYTHM

The word *asceticism* in its original meaning refers to shaping or sculpting something. In its early use in Christian spirituality, it referred to shaping our lives into something beautiful for God. "Ascetical" practices help us in sculpting and shaping.

An asceticism of time management begins in taking the time to reflect on how we structure our days and our weeks. It will include a recovery of space in our day for activities such as recreational time with loved ones and quiet time with God.

The intention of an asceticism of time is not an escape from time, but the saving of time, the transformation of it as the medium through and in which we encounter God and other loved ones who transform us. When by grace and effort we rescue ourselves from dissipated and compulsive time, we participate in its salvation and sanctify it.

An exploration of our roots in Judaism offers a rich harvest with regard to sanctified and saving time. For starters, the Sabbath is not just somebody's nice idea, but a command of God given on Mount Sinai.

The Sabbatarian pattern—six days of work, followed by one of rest—is woven deep into the fabric of the Bible. The very first story of Jewish and Christian scriptures—the creation story—climaxes on the seventh day. Having created everything, God rests, and blesses the day, and makes it holy. In this way, God declares as fully as possible just how very good creation is. Resting, God takes pleasure in what has been made.

One of the most distinguished words in the Hebrew scriptures is *qadosh* (holy), a word that more than any other is representative of the mystery and majesty of the divine. What provided the first occasion for its use—a mountain, an altar? *Time.* "And God blessed the seventh day and made it holy [*qadosh*]" (Gen 2:3). Accustomed religious thinking would expect that after heaven and earth have been established, God would create a holy place, a mountain or a spring, whereupon a sanctuary should be erected, but what comes first is the seventh *day*, the Sabbath, holiness in time.

In this brief overview of the Sabbath's development, we see the various facets of meaning that the seventh day holds within itself today:

- cessation from work
- rest and relaxation
- gratitude of a people set free
- communal liturgical celebration as an expression of our thankfulness for God's redemption
- a pledge of the quality of living that awaits us "out of time"

WHAT *SHOULD* HAPPEN ON THE SABBATH?

Praying: Our way of keeping the Lord's Day holy as Christians reflects our distinctive understanding. For us, it has a new dimension: resurrection. God began a new creation with Christ's death and resurrection. Christians transferred their observance from Saturday to Sunday because on this day the future burst into the present. The appropriate response for the early Christians was to celebrate a feast of communion, looking back to Jesus's passion and resurrection and forward to the great banquet that would occur at the end of time. The result has been centuries of Sunday worship. Every Sunday is a little Easter. A time to gather with song and prayer, to hear the Good News proclaimed, and to recognize Christ in the breaking of the bread.

Playing: Celebrating Sunday means enjoying things you wouldn't even think of doing the other days of the week. A fun novel or book of poetry. Lunch with friends. Strolling through an art gallery. Enjoying a special museum exhibit. A picnic in the park. Writing a letter to an appreciated friend.

All of these things close the door on routine and enter into a playful, festival atmosphere of food, fun, and fellowship, rediscovering one another in leisure, laughter, and love. The Sabbath is meant to be the poetry in the prose of the week. Music. Candles. Art. Gardens, Picnics. Bubble baths. Concerts. The seventh day, embraced as a day just for *being*, lifts us out of our patterned living, our "good ruts." It is the salt that keeps the good self-discipline employed on the other six days of the week from rotting.

Rest and Relaxation: We're good at keeping "half-sabbaths." They're a specialty of our culture. We've gone to church but haven't played. Or gone to the stadium but haven't prayed. Leisure and work-life balance are not luxuries. They are necessities for good health, good energy, and good productivity. They are antidotes to chronic stress. There's a cost to always being "on." It's costly to health, energy, and relationships.

We spend six days of every week working out of three verbs: *doing, wanting, having*. The Sabbath is the day when we add a fourth: *being*. Labor is a craft, but genuine rest—the result of an accord of body, mind, and spirit—is an art. To attain a degree of excellence in art, one must accept its discipline.

The spirit of Sabbath living, however, is to rest on the Sabbath *as if all our work were done*. To rest even from the *thought* of labor. To set apart one day a week for freedom, a day for being with ourselves, independent of external obligations. To declare an armistice day in our economic struggles, a day on which we decline to worship before the idols of productivity and efficiency.

This is not a day for *doing*, but for *being*, for giving thanks for all that is and has been freely given. It is immensely difficult for us to give ourselves permission to use time for creative nondoing, for being still, for being silent, for seeking nothing, for "wasting time with God"—and with regularity, not just when our backs are to the wall, and we are too worn out to work at keeping control.

Time with Family and Friends: The Sabbath also affords us the opportunity to make more time and energy available for some quality time with family members and/or with friends. This can find many expressions, and we've already mentioned some of them. What many of us need most is time with loved ones, time devoted to the pleasure of just being together, perhaps while sharing our enjoyment of art, nature, good food, sports. A special meal—prepared ahead of time with family or friends. There is also a long tradition of visiting the homebound or inviting someone who's lonely to our table on the Sabbath.

For those of you who are already retired, the question becomes: How can I make one day in seven really different from the other six? Break the routine. Do something special. Get together with friends or family.

The spirit of the Sabbath invites us to do things we really enjoy. For me, a good Sabbath day is something like this. No morning alarm clock; just letting myself wake up when I've had enough sleep. And after meditating, getting on my bike and heading off in the morning sunlight for an hour-and-a-half ride to and around local parks, with prayer flowing out of me spontaneously as I pedal and coast. And when I come to a pond, I stop and watch the turtles enjoying an utterly peaceful Sabbath morning setting. And once back home, enjoy the warm water of a shower, dress for Sunday morning Mass, and worship the Lord of the Sabbath. Afterward, I would enjoy brunch with a friend or take a bowl of cereal out to the terrace and listen to the birdsong in the surrounding trees. Then, in the afternoon, I would bring the church/city newspaper and accumulated periodicals outside and enjoy some reading time in the fresh air. It all makes for a rejuvenating Sabbath, leaving me feeling very peaceful and grateful for the many blessings.

An acquaintance of mine, Vanessa White, coordinator of spiritual formation at Xavier University in Los Angeles, wrote, "For my Sabbath, I turn off the cell phone, unplug the computer, turn off the TV, prepare a meal, read from one of my spiritual guides, spend time with family or friends, or just take a walk. I find that after taking the Sabbath time, I return to my daily activities renewed, refreshed, and ready to continue the work the Lord has given me. Taking the time for Sabbath reminds me of the beauty God created, the wonder of the universe, and the goodness that dwells all around."

Chapter 23

MONTHLY POUSTINIA DAY

Poustinia, which comes from the Russian word for "desert," is oftentimes simply referred to as a "desert day." It's part of the Christian Orthodox tradition of seeking solitude in order to remove the distractions that often push to the side our relationship with God. The idea is drawn from Mark 6:31 in which God calls us to a deserted place that is free of distractions so that God can speak more directly to our heart, enabling our relationship to grow.

One doesn't of course have to travel to an actual desert. One can simply seek silence and solitude in a little-used room of the house. That said, we have to admit that there are so many home distractions that breaking free can demand a more radical action, like going to a cottage or retreat house, bringing your Bible and your journal along with you. One can simplify it further by making it a day of fasting as well.

This monthly "rendezvous" can be very helpful in maintaining commitment to and catching the drift in your spiritual practices before that drift gets too far and calling yourself to one or the other of the practices anew.

In a meeting with my spiritual director, I once came with the question, "How much is too much (work), and when does a no to more work give greater glory to God than a yes?"

The line of his response was, "If you're bored by your work, that's one thing. But if you're fed and energized by it, if it's what you live for, that's another thing. When you're a member of an apostolic society of life, and you're living out of your God-given gifts, the invitations that come are the Lord's call to you. Respond with joy for the opportunity to serve. The fact that you feel like you're firing on all cylinders, that your health is good and sustaining, is confirmation that things are fine. If it's not broke, don't fix it, and when you are aware that you're tired and need to rest, arrange for back-up and take the time."

All in all, what he was saying made sense to me. It's what I've been doing. But I raised the question because I was feeling tired of the constant deadlines; every hour in the day is counted and calculated for getting things done, and after a while that wears one down. He was glad to hear that I have tried to build in the "rest stops" with twice daily meditation, a weekly Sabbath, a monthly Poustinia day, and an annual retreat. He said he would give the Poustinia a "ten" on a scale of one to ten in terms of its potential for keeping one anchored and rejuvenated in the Lord. "Examine your calendar and mark it in," he said "You've got the disciplines in place that you should have. Just be faithful in practicing them." And he was glad to hear that I had ten days of vacation coming up! "Hopefully it will be a time of rest, relaxation, and rejuvenation in body, mind, and spirit," he said. I couldn't have said it better!

Over the years I have tried to keep in place a monthly Poustinia (desert/slow down) day away for some quality time with the Lord. But there is often something that crowds out, overlaps, or eats into part of it. Keeping a whole day open just for *being with* is really difficult. There are always so many things *to do*—an article to write, a book to read, a homily to prepare.

One year, the day I had marked off in my calendar for it in the month of March brought its own special temptation. When I rolled out of bed in the morning at the retreat house where I was staying and opened the curtains, what I saw was freshly fallen snow lying under sparkling sunshine and blue sky. Wow, I thought, what a perfect day for cross-country skiing! Could I integrate this into the spirit of the day? Yes, I decided, I could. It would be something fun that celebrates the givenness and giftedness of life. I decided to go for it with passion, just for the morning, and then return for a quiet afternoon.

So, after a quick breakfast, I pulled on my cross-country ski togs, threw the gear in the car, and zoomed off toward the park with the cross-country ski trails. When I looked at the speedometer and saw that I was going too fast, I started to cut back on my speed—

but too late. Next to the highway sat a patrol car with its radar on. Sure enough, he pulled out, "on" went his flashers, and he pulled in behind me and signaled me over.

As he was writing me out a speeding ticket, I realized I felt more upset with myself for contravening my own rule: Don't hurry. You can't force things. Live deliberately in loving attention with the Lord. I needed slowing down, and the police officer did it. By the time he returned from his car with the ticket, I was pretty sure what I was going to do. A glance at the $42 fine on the ticket helped seal the decision. I accepted it as a penance for my failure to keep my own code of slowing down and living more deliberately. I started up the car, took the first exit I came to, and slowly drove back to the retreat house. I went to my room, changed clothes, and went out for a quiet walk in the woods with the Lord, stopping to listen to the bird's early song of spring, to feel the sun warm on my face, to breathe deeply and taste the delicious quality of the air.

I thanked the Lord for slowing me down. "Letting my skis carve alleluias in the snow would have been nice, but let's face it: a quiet focused day with You should be just that! When I start 'selling out' on it to other, competing offers, pull me over and fine me, Lord; $42 is a small price to pay if I finally learn my lesson."

People get at different times an intuition of where their joy is. When you get into it, it's like discovering a trail that's been there all the time waiting for you, and there's a sense of being helped by invisible hands to stay on it. The point is that the waters of eternal life are right there, wherever you are, if you're following your bliss.

I spent the rest of the day reflecting on and responding to these questions:

What values, virtues, qualities do I want to embody, in and through my choices and myself?

The value of the gift of life. The virtue of gratitude. The quality of living deliberately.

What do I want to do with my life when all is said and done?

Become a person who lives with a sense of the sacredness of all life; who lives wrapped in a sense of mystery; who responds with awe and wonder.

When do I feel best about myself?

When I respond to needs beyond myself, transcend my own self-centered preoccupations, and am drawn out of myself and thus forget myself or serve the needs of others.

What is fulfilling for me to do?

Things that strengthen or express my deepest aspirations: celebrating the Eucharist, helping the needy, meditating, reading, writing, preaching, sharing with friends.

When have I been so fully engrossed in an activity that time/ space were lost on me?

This happens consistently in writing. There is no other activity in which time so collapses and the hours just fly by.

In what ways do I feel particularly called to grow at the present time?

By easing my foot on the accelerator of daily tasks and slowing down into a simpler life. In short, as noted above, the quality of deliberate living. Break my work-compulsive pattern where all time is organized around work concerns. This choice is designed to give me more personal time for vital activities that help me live a more centered, aware life. To close the door on routine and enter more into a playful festive atmosphere of food, fun, and fellowship, rediscovering one another in leisure and laughter.

We need to make our lives more poetic with art, music, flowers, candles, incense, picnics, and bubble baths. Breaking the pattern of our day with poetry and play is the salt that keeps good self-discipline from rotting.

Having a truly Sabbath day each week is important. Celebrating Sunday does not mean simply going to church and staying out of the office to recover energy to work again in the weekdays. It means living in the presence of God more consciously. The weekdays are for the sake of the Sabbath, which is not an interlude but the climax of living. It's a day in which to truly practice *mindfulness*.

Let it begin with awakening and lying in bed in the morning, beginning with slow, long, and conscious breaths. Then slowly rise from bed, and once up, go to the bathroom, wash/shave/shower slowly and mindfully, each action being done in a calm and relaxing way, so that by the time you are finished, you feel light and refreshed. When preparing a meal, do so slowly and calmly, enjoying each mouthful and truly sipping the drink. Just live the moment. Over the course of the day, read some scripture, sit in meditation, take a slow walk in a nearby park. When each Sabbath truly becomes a day of slow-down mindfulness, it will have a positive effect on the way we live the other days of the week as well.

Chapter 24

YOGA PRAYER

The doctrine of the Incarnation is at the heart of Christian faith. It's about the second person of the Trinity coming down from heaven and entering fully into the human condition in the life and death of Jesus of Nazareth. It is not so much that the one who came to be referred to as the Word entered into the world; it is rather that the Word became *flesh*. In short, God personally identified with our "bodiliness," fleshiness, materiality, and sensuality, leaving us with no right to dismiss the material world as some second-rate practice field for the real life in heaven.

In short, we have not been burdened with this world and this flesh in order that we might weasel our way out; rather, we have been *gifted* with this world and these bodies because this is where God dwells. All flesh is holy. It is in these bodies that we work out our salvation. Our corporeal nature is the place that God chose to call "home."

During my monthlong retreat in 1991 at Shantivanam Christian ashram in India, I discovered a concrete application of my incarnational faith in their daily yoga session followed by meditation. The use of bodily postures to open us to God is already well-established in Christian practice worldwide, for example, kneeling down invites our mind and heart to be prayerfully present. At our community worship, we stand to express our dignity and shared mission, kneel to express the transcendence of God, and touch one another at the sign of peace to recognize our bondedness in the Holy Spirit. Depending on what church one enters on Sunday, one will find a range of other bodily postures expressing openness to God: genuflecting, bowing, and kissing icons, sitting quietly with open hands, standing with hands raised high toward heaven, and prostration. Gesture obviously unites mind and body and presents us in a holistic way to God.

Today, many Christians are finding in hatha yoga and other practices the help that they have been looking for in order to live more fully an incarnational Christian faith that values the human body as a divine gift. And yes, I have met Christians along the way who are wary of yoga because of its origination in other religious contexts. But God seems often pleased to show us the divine handiwork in the lives of those who belong to other religious paths in order that our faith convictions may remain humble and nonjudgmental and truly open to the Spirit of God at work everywhere in the world.

The Vatican's "Letter to the Bishops of the Catholic Church on Some Aspects of Christian Meditation"[1] was motivated by an increasing contact of Christians with other religions and with their different styles and methods of prayer. It mentioned in particular the Eastern methods of Zen, transcendental meditation, and yoga. It responds to the question of what value these forms of prayer or preparation for prayer might have for Christians:

> The majority of the great religions which have sought union with God in prayer have also pointed out ways to achieve it. Just as the "Catholic Church rejects nothing of what is true and holy in these religions" (Vatican II's Decree on Non-Christians, no. 2), neither should these ways be rejected out of hand simply because they are not Christian. On the contrary, one can take from them what is useful so long as the Christian conception of prayer, its logic and requirements are never obscured.

The irrefutable proof that yoga is not a religion and not necessarily tied to Hindu philosophical convictions is simply the facts on the ground: today Jews, Buddhists, Christians, Muslims, and people of no particular religious affiliation, all—in addition to Hindus—practice hatha yoga.

THE CONNECTION BETWEEN MEDITATION AND YOGA

My few months of sabbatical in India provided me with a meaningful experience of this practice because it was rooted in restoring the original connection between meditation and yoga and helping Christians to plant both in the soil of their own faith.

I had been meditating for sixteen years before experiencing the beneficial effects of yoga in preparing one for meditation. Earlier, I had heard that yoga helps one to meditate better, so I gave it a try and found that it was true. Yoga is first and foremost a practical spiritual discipline. That said, it's important to know that there are many different kinds of yoga out there today, stemming either from the classical or the contemporary tradition.

In the classical tradition, its goal is to center, ground, make present and aware, to create an inner climate of receptivity, whereas in the contemporary tradition, it's all about fitness and using yoga as a form of exercise. The contemporary tradition's focus is more on workout, flexibility, coordination, posture, balance, relaxation—all positive benefits, but in the classical scheme of things, secondary.

How can yoga enrich the life of a Christian or member of any religion? By balancing the nervous system and stilling the mind. In short, by creating an environment in the body for meditation. The sixteenth-century Spanish mystic Teresa of Avila speaks in her writings on prayer about "the fool in the house"—the restless mind. If you've ever tried to meditate, you know what she's talking about.

In the classical tradition, what is known as hatha yoga was originally designed to help people to meditate better by helping them to develop stronger backs and more flexible hips and knees so as to be able to sit in the cross-legged position with a straight back for longer periods of time to soak in the mystery of their immortal soul. In short, to help people to sit in meditation comfortably, with a calmer body and quieter, more focused mind.

Interestingly, a growing number of Christian teachers of yoga today are making a contribution to restoring this connection by teaching, along with yoga, a method for meditation drawn from the Christian tradition of contemplative prayer. In my own book *Prayer of Heart and Body: Meditation and Yoga as Christian Spiritual Practice*, the prayer of the body is yoga and the prayer of the heart is meditation. I regard them as twins joined at the head. As appreciable as the physical benefits are, they're still just half a loaf. The stability referred to by the physical practice of asanas (postures) relates to mental as well as physical stability.

The contraction and relaxation of the muscles with deep breathing unload tension and stress from the body-mind, enabling you to sit calm and quiet in your body with a focused mind in meditation. Where you point the mind will be shaped by your own faith tradition and understanding. One of the things that makes the practice attractive to North Americans is that it gives fidgety activists something to do that has a calming effect. It is a systematic program for peaceful living with sharpened self-awareness and a positive and comprehensive approach to holistic health through the integration of body, mind, and spirit. As such, it is a valuable instrument to promote one's spiritual well-being.

While it has an Eastern origin, yoga transcends both cultural and geographical boundaries that initially supported it. It is not necessarily tied to Hindu cultural expressions or even Hindu philosophical understandings. Thus it has become a valued practice/instrument in the lives of people from all religions or none.

CHRISTIANS PRACTICING YOGA

In 2001, I offered a retreat for Christian yoga instructors at what was then a Paulist retreat center in Oak Ridge, New Jersey. It was an affirming and energizing experience for all, and they asked, "Can we come together like this again?"

When I look back on how this all began, I simply fall silent and bow my head before the work of the Holy Spirit, starting with the yoga classes at Shantivanam in India in 1991. Upon my return, I eventually went for teacher training and certification in 1993–94 at the Kripalu yoga center in Massachusetts. Afterward, through the classes and retreats I began to offer at the Unitas spirituality center in Montreal, Quebec, from 1994 to 1999, a network of teachers we called "Oak Ridge" took root and began to grow through an every-other-year summer retreat. In the first Oak Ridge retreat gathering in 2001, there were eighteen participants. In 2003, twenty-five. In 2005, thirty-four. In 2007, forty. The network of Christian teachers of yoga has just kept on growing via the group's website.[2]

The teachers came to these retreats from Texas, California, Oregon, Fort Macmurray, and Alberta in the west, to New Hampshire, Massachusetts, Maryland, Connecticut, New York, New Jersey, Pennsylvania, DC, and Alabama in the east, and parts in between like Ontario, Quebec, Michigan, and Minnesota. From these far-flung places they came to the retreat center situated on a spring-fed lake in the woods in northern New Jersey for a five-day experience to deepen and strengthen their faith and their spiritual practice. When that retreat center was sold and became a school, the network of instructors continued with their bi-annual retreat in various other retreat locations.

In 2014–15, I led a group of twenty-five on a pilgrimage to Shantivanam ashram in India where I had been introduced to yoga in 1991 by the Benedictine monk Fr. Bede Griffith and his ashram community. It was powerful for me to be back in the place where the Lord planted the seeds for a whole new development in my life, writing the *Prayer of Heart and Body*, becoming a yoga instructor, producing a DVD *Yoga Prayer*, and starting what has become an international network of Christian teachers of yoga, whose website is now accessed around the world.

My first experience with yoga and the opportunity to practice it linked to meditation happened in the Shantivanam Christian ashram. The Spirit fertilized and watered the seeds, and they bore fruit for the service of the people of God at a time when yoga was beginning to go mainstream back in North America, but where there were very few Christians making any effort to help all those of Christian background engaging with yoga to do so in a way coherent with their own faith.

It also coincided with my ecumenical ministry, as it drew Christians from different churches together in national and international retreats. It not only enriched and enlarged my way of praying as a Christian but also exemplified that there is a lot of heat and light in what is called "spiritual ecumenism," which involves the exchange of spiritual gifts, personal holiness of life, and inner conversion. At Oak Ridge, we became a praying community of people from mainline churches and free churches, from southern and northern, eastern and western churches, interweaving embodied yoga prayer and meditative prayer.

To realize that yoga is not in itself a religion, simply look at who practices it: Hindus, Buddhists, Jains, Jews, Christians, and people of no religious affiliation.

Think of it as a software to be plugged into the hardware of your own faith understanding and to be worked with in a way that accords with that understanding.

As Georg Feuerstein, the founder and director of the Yoga Research Institute in California and the author of the encyclopedia of the yoga tradition says, "You don't have to accept Hindu/Buddhist/Jain philosophical or religious tenets to practice yoga. You only have to believe you can go beyond your present egocentric state of existence." Feuerstein's counsel: Practicing Christians or Jews (or practitioners of any other religious tradition) should take from yoga what makes sense to them and deepens their own faith and spiritual commitment. In other words, it is a software that you can plug into the hardware of your own faith understanding and work with accordingly.

So, yes, yoga can and in fact has been and is practiced by people with widely differing philosophies and beliefs. The facts on the ground make that clear. There are classes for Orthodox Jews in New York City. There are Muslim instructors in Washington, DC, and there's a growing network of Christian teachers of yoga in many cities around the country. The network that has evolved from the seeds planted in my first retreat for Christian teachers of yoga back in 2000 is entering a new evolutionary phase—it's become a non-profit corporation!

What others need to understand and accept is that it is incumbent on Christians working with disciplines like yoga or Zen or Tai Chi to apply to their practice a Christian understanding. The understanding that distinguishes the Christian approach to a spiritual practice or method is not that one will achieve union with God by dint of one's own effort, but that through the practice one will put oneself in the place or provide the opening where God's grace can effectively enter in and do its healing, transforming, and unifying work. Furthermore, what makes a particular practice Christian is not its source, but its intent. If one's intent in assuming a particular practice is to deepen awareness in Christ, then it is Christian.

Many Christians appreciate this spiritual practice because our faith so highly esteems our embodied nature. At Christmas, we celebrate God becoming flesh in the historical person of Jesus of Nazareth. At Easter, we celebrate the *bodily* resurrection. On the Feast of the Ascension, we celebrate Jesus's *bodily* ascension into heaven. On Pentecost, we celebrate the Holy Spirit poured into these vessels of clay that we are. In short, our bodies are instruments and receptacles of grace. So, it should not surprise us that Christians, with their very "enfleshed spirituality," might feel at home in and with a spiritual practice that provides a way of going to God the way God came to us—in and through a body.

Chapter 25

EXPERIENCING GOD IN NATURE

I am a lover of the outdoors. My experiences in the glories of nature are among those that remain the most deeply etched in my soul. A good example would be that of the opportunities I have had to hike in the mountains. Visits to one of my friends in Switzerland who has a chalet in the Alps has offered marvelous experiences. On one of my occasions there, I set off from the alpine cabin about 8:00 a.m. to hike up the mountain to Lake Tsaté, intending to return for lunch around noon. But along the way, the Lord spoke to my heart and soul through the silence and vastness of the mountains, the fragility and sheer gratuity of the gloriously colored wildflowers that have no other purpose in this world than to glorify their Creator, and by so doing fulfill the reason for their being.

Once at Lake Tsaté in the open Alpine meadow surrounded by peaks and with a marvelous view across the valley, I felt in my heart the Lord's calling me to this "deserted place" and recognized that this was the "desert day" I hoped to find with him somewhere along the way in my vacation. Like everything else, it was given and exceeded my wildest imaginings. I sat and read a chapter from a pocket-sized gospel, and afterward, decided to climb higher to the peak, taking my time, saying the Jesus prayer. The closing line in the chapter I had just read was "I live now, not I, but Christ lives in me." My prayer was "live me, Lord," and I reflected on the mystery of that phrase as I climbed.

At the peak, there was a magnificent view of both sides of the divide. I stayed there awhile meditating on what I was seeing. God, through time, churns out enormity to beat into our heads that we are in a world not of our own making. The only one who is always and everywhere at home in it is God. The rest of us are strangers and pilgrims. In all directions soared peaks hundreds of thousands of years old, and to my right and left moved inchingly each day two enormous glaciers, gouging out in their turn a landscape that those coming here a thousand years from now would look at in wonder.

Another climber indicated to me that if I really wanted to see all there was to see, that I should climb yet higher. So, I made my way without benefit of trail from 2,800 meters to 3,000 meters. There, I was reduced to utter muteness within and without. Never have I had a 360-degree view that so inspired awe, that spoke so powerfully of the tremendous and fascinating mystery of God's creation.

On the way down, I lay in the grass among the wildflowers in the meadow at Lake Tsaté and, with the sun beating full upon my face, entered into a river of praise raised up by the Spirit of God within me. When I descended the mountain path, the late-afternoon quality of light was so soft and translucent, the color of the sky such a delicious blue and the cloud formations so varied behind the breathtaking range of peaks in front of me. The whole of it was a festival of color, form, and light that filled me with the sheer joy of being. I felt so blessed to experience, witness, see, touch, feel, the overwhelmingly munificent outpouring of God's manifest presence in creation.

They were days full of awe and wonder, and the mind-blowing experience of beauty left no room for back-home concerns thousands of miles away. There is nothing like a hike in the mountains to help one keep small things small. In this experience of the One in whom all years and months are an eternal now, came the words: "All shall be well, and all shall be well, and all manner of things shall be well."

CROSS-COUNTRY SKIING

Another thing I love to do out-of-doors is cross-country skiing. During my twenty-two years in Montreal, I lived in a residence just a block or so from Mount Royal Park, which in the wintertime had groomed cross-country ski trails up and down and all around the mountain. Regularly getting out for an early-morning ski was for me a form of morning prayer, of giving glory to God for the marvels of creation.

One of my clergy buddies, Fr. Anthony Randazzo, and I also enjoyed some blissful days in Vermont. We once enjoyed a week's vacation together at the Craftsbury Outdoor Center in Vermont, a place that offers a rented cabin, three meals a day, and use of groomed out-of-the-wind cross-country ski trails in the woods. At the end of a day of gliding prayer on the trails, the hike up the hill to the dining hall by the light of the full moon for a halibut supper with pecans, Indian beans, rice, and an apple crisp dessert made for an "off-the-charts" day! And in the evening, we'd go for a walk on the frozen lake under the full moon before enjoying some relaxing conversation by the warmth of the fireplace. At the end of the time, all I could say was, "Thank you, Lord, for the gift of life!"

RAPTURE

The theologian would call it
"realized eschatology,"
the whirling dervish,
"ecstasy,"
the renunciate in saffron robes,
"bliss."

It comes with the glide
of cross-country skis
in freshly fallen snow,

with the deep diaphragm inhalation
of invigorating air
as your arms and shoulders pump
in rhythm with hip-driven legs.

It comes when the swishing stops
in the middle of the forest
and you listen to your soul-song
wafting up into the pines

or when you stand in a field
and survey the dunes of white
sculptured by the wind.

It's an ethereal, psychic zone
to which the body gives full access,
an experience the skier would call
rapture.

With each new day, we just dressed for warmth, hit the trails, and skied for hours. It's mysterious to me how jubilant I feel gliding through the forest or standing in the midst of an open field in the cold, blowing wind. I'm amazed by how good my body feels in this practice! I do workout regularly, but thirty to forty minutes isn't five hours! Cross-country skiing gives me a flowing fountain of energy. The air tastes so delicious in my deep lungs, and the woods are so lovely, quiet, and deep. Anthony and I also meditate together in the morning, celebrate the Eucharist in the late afternoon, and meditate again after holy communion before heading off for good conversation over supper. In the evening we take some time to read by the fireplace and have a look at the day's email, then to bed.

It helps one find a better balance in living. The combination of physical exercise, delicious food, good conversations about church and ministry around the fireplace in the cabin, meditating and celebrating Eucharist together, an hour of reading, Wi-fi for keeping up with email—a combination both refreshing and renewing in spirit and body.

NEWFOUNDLAND

Another place of awesome beauty in the northeast is the Canadian province of Newfoundland. I had the opportunity to explore it by adding on a few days of vacation time following retreats I was invited to lead in various areas there. The entire province is a forest laced with rivers and decorated with lakes. On my first time there, when I was picked up at the airport by one of the Sisters, the drive to the retreat center in Grand Falls was like being in the Boundary Water Canoe Area of northern Minnesota, only in a car instead of a canoe.

When the retreat ended, I headed for what became one of my favorite places on the planet: Gros Morne National Park on Newfoundland's west coast. I stayed at a bed and breakfast at Woody Point in the park, a 105-year-old house with white-lace curtains and colorful handmade quilts on the bed. At breakfast, Ruth asked me if there were any moose where I lived. "No," I said, smiling even at the thought of a moose in Washington, DC. "I had a moose and her calf in my garden last week," she said.

Gros Morne, a World Heritage Site covering 1,800 square kilometers, is a never-ending series of wonders and delights and a demonstration of the indescribable raw and enigmatic beauty of the physical world. I had only forty hours there before having to head back to the airport, but I took five spectacular hikes—one to the top of a mountain; another along cliffs overlooking the sea; another on the Tablelands (upthrust from the ocean floor when two continents collided 1.5 billion years ago); another hike on the beach, exploring sea caves and waterfalls from the forest; and a final jaunt through the woods along a lake. The geological diversity takes one's breath away. I also enjoyed a hike to Lookout Point, which offered its own spectacular views. The following day, I set out to hike the Green Gardens trail, arriving at the sea and beach for low tide. There I found the sea cave and walked back to the waterfalls, taking pictures of the sea stacks. The glories of God's creation incited my spirit to rise up and dance!

The night before I flew out, two nuns, both of whom had been on the retreat, offered me the guest room in their house in Deer Lake. The church's secretary, Elizabeth Ryan, said she had traced her branch of the Ryan family back to 1720 in Newfoundland. She said that just about everybody in the province can trace their ancestry back to Ireland. One of the things that I love about the "Newfies" is that they are so simple and genuine and hospitable. My flight was leaving at 6:00 a.m., and that meant being picked up by a cab at 4:30 a.m. I said goodnight to the Sisters about 9:30 p.m. and thanked them for their hospitality and told them I would just slip out quietly in the morning. But when I came down the next morning, there they both were, fully dressed, with a pot of "farewell tea" on the stove, ready to be poured. After a couple of days of rest and relaxation in Grose Morne and such local hospitality, all I could say was, "Thank you, Lord, for all the blessings of the week and for your marvelous creation."

Part Six

TRAVEL

A Missionary's Life

After being ordained a priest, my first five years were stable and devoted to campus ministry in two years at Ohio State University and three at McGill University in Montreal, Quebec. Once I joined the team at the Montreal-based Canadian Centre for Ecumenism (CCE), however, the rhythm-and-flow of life changed. It wasn't long before I would be in good measure "on the road" ministering in all ten provinces of Canada.

While ongoing travel can be taxing, it also has its benefits. At the top of my list of benefits during my fourteen years at the CCE was the opportunity to experience the cultural diversity and the natural geographical splendor of Canada's ten provinces—the glorious mountains of British Columbia and Alberta; the lakes, rivers, and prairies of Saskatchewan and Manitoba; the hills, lakes, and forests of Ontario and Quebec; the beaches, boating, and fishing of New Brunswick, Nova Scotia, Prince Edward Island, and Newfoundland. During all my years in Montreal, I lived just a block from Mount Royal Park in the heart of the city, which gave me a much-enjoyed opportunity in the winter months to regularly engage in my favorite sport—cross-country skiing. I became a dual citizen with citizenship in both the United States and Canada.

My ecumenical and interfaith ministry occasioned a significant amount of national and international travel to participate in assemblies, conferences, and dialogues. In 1983, the year my responsibilities increased from associate directorship to becoming the director of the Canadian Centre for Ecumenism, the World Council of Churches General Assembly was held in Vancouver, British Columbia, Canada.

The theme of the 1983 assembly in Vancouver was "Jesus Christ, the Life of the World"; 850 representatives from around the world attended the assembly. Some of the work tackled the problem of peace at a time of the nuclear arms race. The theme of "Justice, Peace, and the Integrity of Creation" with its protection of the environment also started to emerge and would receive more attention in future assemblies.

The World Council of Churches (WCC), based in Geneva, Switzerland, is a Christian ecumenical organization founded in 1948 in Amsterdam as "a fellowship of Churches which accept Jesus Christ our Lord as God and Saviour." The WCC is not a church, nor does it issue orders or directions to the churches. It works for the unity and renewal of the Christian denominations and offers them a forum in which they may work together in the spirit of tolerance and mutual understanding.

As time rolled on, to deepen my experience of life and worship in other Christian traditions, I made a month-long pilgrimage to European sacred sites, churches, and monasteries in Vienna, Salzburg, Budapest, Bucharest, Moldavia, Sofia, Athens, Paros, and Patmos.

During my travels, the reading of the gospels became an ongoing source of inspiration. I could spend an hour on a single chapter in intermittent reflection, just stopping and starting, with many of the verses revealing something fresh, like I'd never read it that way before. For example, in chapter 24 of Luke's gospel, Jesus comes off as being in constant dialogue with the Father, as though he lives in the consciousness of the Father's presence: "Father, let this cup pass from me....Father, forgive them, for they know not what they do.... Father, into your hands I place my spirit."

In my own small way, especially when I travel, I have a similar experience with Jesus, perhaps because I often depend on God's providence for safety, lodging, nourishment. Hence I find that travel contributes to my sense of deepening relationship with the Lord simply because there is more communication. In the absence of someone else, he becomes more consciously a companion presence, and many thoughts, reactions, feelings get expressed directly to him. I may be traveling alone, but I do not have the sense of *being alone*.

At the end of a day, that sense of presence finds expression in journal entries like, "I want to know you, Lord, know you personally, directly, deeply. I want to feel the fire of your zeal for the spread of the reign of God in people's hearts and lives. I want you to bring me out of 'mediocre' into 'radical,' beyond 'measured' to 'not counting the cost.' I want you to teach me the meaning of whole-hearted commitment, of giving my all."

Chapter 26

GREECE, HUNGARY, ROMANIA, AND RUSSIA

GREECE

It was May 1983 and Holy Week in Greece, but Athens was hot and noisy, and on the "littered" side. It is probably the only place in Greece where people *do* rush, so I had no desire to stay there very long. I was hearing the siren call of the islands and decided to head for Paros. The people on the ferry were geared for pleasure. We arrived in Paroikia, the capital village of Paros, and took a bus to Naoussa, a sleepy little fishing village on one end of the island.

Everybody in Paros goes to church on Sunday. I had never seen such a display of religious solidarity. It seemed likely that everybody in Naoussa was Orthodox. There were whole families present: women on one side, men on the other, children down the center aisle. But out of that whole packed church, only the babes in arms received communion! In the Roman Catholic church going to communion is by and large taken-for-granted, but in these Orthodox countries that's by no means the case. I was surprised at the convent of Varatec to see only a few Sisters take communion. I asked Mother Nazaria about this, and she said that generally they will receive twice during Lent, and maybe eight to ten times across the whole of the year. These are church members who spend about half of every day in church praying. I had difficulty reconciling this in the Byzantine practice with the spiritual dimension of the Eucharist as meal.

My desire was to spend the Holy Week Triduum on the island of Patmos. It is frequently said that the Greek Orthodox consider themselves a little more authentic than any other national Orthodox church. Undoubtedly because the culture that went out to all the other churches under the rubrics of the Byzantine Rite was Hellenistic—and that makes them nearer to the well of inspiration than any other culture.

The liturgies of Holy Week were distressingly passive experiences for me. There were only four or five people who actually did anything—the priest and four cantors. Everybody else just sat there for a couple of hours without a spoken response or a sung response. The people of course are expected to be praying interiorly along with the singers, but for me it was an experience of liturgical minimalism at best. Liturgy, as a "work of the people" was lost a few hundred years ago when the singing was usurped by a few professionally trained cantors out of a sense that the melodies were too complicated for the people to handle. Worship in the monasteries, however, is a very different experience because there most everyone is singing and making frequent *metanias*—a sign of the cross with a deep bow. But the liturgies, albeit formed in the monasteries, do not always translate very successfully into the parishes. One thing in particular is impressive though: everybody comes—children, young adults, parents, and the elderly.

The Latin liturgy was not that different until the 1922 *Missa recitata* ("Dialogue Mass"), which restored dialogue to the eucharistic liturgy in religious houses. The priest turned toward the people for the prayer exchange, and people loved it even though it was in Latin. Gradually over the next couple of decades or so, the whole Roman Catholic Church began to use missals at Mass and respond in dialogue to the celebrant. Not surprisingly, people wondered "Why not pray in the vernacular (English)?" Now in the Roman church a much more active role on the part of congregants is taken for granted. The liturgical movement prepared the church for renewal throughout the first half of the twentieth century, leading up to the Second Vatican Council in the early 1960s in which the first document passed was The Constitution on the Sacred Liturgy.

PATMOS

The Greeks were heading for the islands en masse to celebrate Easter. My own destination was the island of Patmos, where the apostle John lived for a time and died. I made the twelve-hour boat trip to the island a retreat day, just sitting and reading and reflecting on John's gospel, as well as his three short letters prior to his Book of Revelation. The relationship of John with God his Father came through in technicolor, and it was as though I'd only "seen it" in black and white before. The blessing I was moved to ask for in my pilgrimage to this holy place was that the scriptures be increasingly a living word for me, a daily bread.

Our boat got in about midnight, and I went to a Good Friday service in the morning at St. John's parish church in Sala, the lower town in Patmos, and then hiked an hour up to the upper town, Chora, stopping regularly to be blown away by the view. I then visited the cave where John is said to have written the Book of Revelations, and went from there to the monastery of St. John, perched like a fortress on the very acme of Chora.

The major Good Friday service took place at 8:00 p.m. After three hours of chanting, the funeral bier, wonderfully decorated with roses—white, red, pink, orange, and rose—and orchids, and containing the embroidered image of Christ laid in the tomb, was carried in procession through the streets. The Good Friday tone is well expressed by the roses and orchids, as the message of the songs is not "Christ has died—beat your breasts," but "Thank you, Lord, for loving and saving us."

On Holy Saturday morning, I returned to the cave of the Apocalypse to read what John had dictated to his scribe of his vision on this spot. Somehow, outside a cave high on a hill overlooking the sea and island, it was not as difficult to enter into the symbolic language of Revelation regarding the cosmic struggle between angels and dragons. In the afternoon, I explored the labyrinthine streets and churches in Chora. It is the Byzantine custom to spread green boughs of evergreen on the floor of the chapels and churches, and when you walk in, there is pleasant shock to the sense of smell.

Outside, the view is spectacular: the peninsular arms of the island with its inland port; the sea and islands beyond; the terraced hillside gradually sloping away to the sun-splashed port village of

Scala below. The blue of the Aegean makes the cloudless sky seem off-white, so deep is its color.

Late in the evening, I hiked up the hill to the monastery for the Easter Vigil, and at 11:00 p.m., the chapel was already packed with people standing in the courtyard outside. The Easter fire was to be lit about midnight. I squeezed my way into the packed chapel, and at midnight when the monks came out and stood in the center of the chapel facing one another, the abbot came through the doors with a paschal candle to proclaim *Christos anesti*! ("Christ is risen!"). Each of us were given by the monks a pure beeswax candle about two feet high and three-quarters of an inch thick. It was clearly a candle designed for the length of the service! Leading up to the abbot's proclamation had been the rhythm of the semantron bells outside the monastery door. Then when the resurrection was proclaimed, the bells began to ring out from both the monastery and the town below, and I could hear the fireworks going off in the port below.

The liturgy leaped and bounded forward with "alleluias" and "Christ is risen from the dead, trampling down death by death, he bestoweth life to those in the tomb" chanted over and over again. Everyone stood with candles aglow both within and without the chapel, and the two chandeliers that hung from the chapel ceiling had some thirty candles each, creating a warm glow that sent lively shadows dancing on the walls painted with figures of the saints, seemingly causing them to sway to the rhythm of the energized chanting. The liturgy lasted until 2:00 a.m. and the chapel easily contained those of us who were still there at the end. Many of the Greeks seemed to check out sometime after the fireworks to go home to a festive meal.

I received communion—a first for me in an Orthodox service—but everything within and without was a green light. It had been a long pilgrimage to celebrate Easter in this place, and after close to three weeks in Orthodox churches along the way, with much participation in their services but no holy communion, I was primed. In walking back to my overnight lodging, I saw through windows Greek families seated around the table for their Easter meal.

On Easter Sunday, I heard music coming from the port area and could see people dancing on the roof of the Port Police building. When I walked over and climbed the staircase to the roof, the tourist police were there offering a meal of pascal lamb with Greek salads and beer, free for all who wished to come. The music was live and I entered readily into the dance of life. As it neared 3:00 p.m., the party started to break up and people began climbing the hill toward the monastery for the Service of Love and Forgiveness. The monks' singing was even more full of energy than the night before, and it was evident that they were in good spirits. At the end of the service, the abbot stood in the holy doors of the iconostasis and handed out red Easter eggs to everyone.

On Easter Monday, because the Feast of St. John corresponded with Easter Sunday on the Byzantine church calendar that year, the celebration of the feast day—an important one for this island dedicated to him—was deferred to Monday. It took place at the little chapel of St. John on the beach, constructed on the site where the villagers were baptized by the apostle. Those who could crowded into the chapel and those who could not stayed without. At the end of the liturgy, huge chunks of blessed bread (not holy communion) were distributed to all present.

It started to rain lightly around noon, and a family waved to me to come join them under their porch roof for their Easter meal of roast lamb and grilled octopus. Their Greek style of holiday meal seemed to be, not to sit down at a set table, but to tear apart and cut up the lamb, eating a piece of it while walking around in and out of the house, from the porch to the terrace, waving a shank bone in one hand and a can of beer in the other in animated conversation.

The island has numerous hiking trails, and some of the most interesting parts of the island can only be reached on foot. After taking an afternoon walking tour of the various bays and beaches overshadowed by high, rising hills, I returned to the village of Scala by 6:00 p.m., where Greek folk-dancing was beginning in the town square. At tables lining the square, a free meal of lamb, potatoes, rice, bread, and retsina was being given to everyone. The square was decorated with colored bunting, and soon the dancers—about thirty men and women, boys and girls, all dressed in various folk costumes, wove their way through the crowd and began to dance.

The abbot and monks from the monastery were given seats of honor alongside the town officials. The town fiddler played along with two others, a lute and a kind of stringed keyboard with xylophone sticks. Always, in the background, the cherry bombs lit by the young people were dropped randomly here and there. Although it scared the wits out of many a bystander, it seemed to be tolerated by the Greek adults as part of the ritual of these days. When the dancers finished their hour-long rendition, the pavement was turned over to the spectators, now turned dancers, as the fiddler played on.

On Easter Tuesday the monks in the monastery had a procession of icons and relics through the streets of the local village of Chora. They came out of the monastery church dressed in robes of various rich colors, carrying relics of the saints from their monastery treasury and great icons, some of them three feet by three feet, requiring two people to carry them. As the procession wove down the streets toward the town square, people came out of their houses with flower-bedecked icons of their own and joined in the procession.

Once gathered in the village square, there were several chants, followed by the blessing of the water font, which was trimmed in roses and palm branches. The people then came up one by one to the abbot for a sprinkling on their head with the blessed water. The abbot sprinkled with a tightly knit large hand corsage of multicolored roses, dipping them now and again in the font. All those with icons—big and small, ancient and new—formed a circle on the perimeter of the square, and everyone moved around in procession inside their circle, kissing the icons and signing themselves with the sign of the cross.

Then the monks split up with small groups of icon-bearers and went to different neighborhoods of the village to enter the houses and bless them. All the doors of the village were opened, awaiting a blessing. After receiving it, the woman of the house sprinkled with rosewater those who had come. For the Orthodox, the whole of Holy Week is integrated into what is referred to as "a single day."

BUDAPEST, HUNGARY

After Holy Week in Greece, I traveled to Hungary's capital, Budapest, bisected by the river Danube. Its nineteenth-century Chain Bridge connects the hilly Buda district with flat Pest. Walking the streets of Budapest was like looking at a person suffering from malnutrition under whose sunken features one can still easily discern a great beauty or handsomeness. People who are unthinking about war should be sent on a trip through central Europe. Looking at pictures of the St. Stephen's Cathedral in Vienna, with its main body gutted by a direct bomb hit, or the Royal Palace in Budapest, or finding that there is no Old Munich to see anymore because it was all demolished and a modern city rebuilt. These are experiences to make pacifists of unreflective people.

Budapest struck me as a city with feeling. Had I seen it at the turn of the century I might have been more inclined to say it was a city that had passion. But now it was like the wrinkled face and hands of a person who has suffered much. Like the beautiful interior of the defaced building in which I was staying, I didn't doubt the presence of a resilient and strong inner spirit in the Hungarian people. But inner beauty is ideally mirrored exteriorly; and when it is not, it takes more imagination to see it. The soul of any city—it's people—unquestionably animated this place. But the body was scarred—not only with living, as in Rome, but with fighting—and was past its prime. I can think of no greater expression of evil and human sinfulness than war and its causes. I have never known war firsthand, but its proximity in the current Russian invasion of Ukraine brings its horrors up close, inciting grief and sorrow for the death and destruction.

One compelling reason to travel is to see what is left of this lovely planet and its people before we blow it up and further erase the treasure of civilization irrevocably.

BUCHAREST, ROMANIA

From Hungary I went on to neighboring Romania. I was so glad to have the chance to broaden my impressions of Romania. Had I extrapolated from impressions of Bucharest, the capital and commercial center in southern Romania, to the whole of Romania, it would have been unfair and inaccurate. A century ago, the capital of Romania was known as "the Paris of the East" for its French-style art and vibrant cultural life. But between World War II and an earthquake in 1977, the city lost much of that grandeur. During three days in Bucharest, I hardly took any photos, though I love to photograph a trip so as to share it with others. There was simply nothing that compelled me to aim the camera at it. There were some fine facades to certain buildings, but in general the city lacked allure. The images that rest with me are plaster crack, peeling paint, spit on the sidewalks, and block after block of post-earthquake jousting: tall, thin, high-rise apartments that looked like match boxes standing on end all in a row. Today, however, historic hotels have been renovated and the city is gaining a reputation for an active nightlife.

Iași in northeastern Romania and near the border of the former Soviet Union is considered the cultural capital of Romania and is also referred to as Jassy. It is the second largest city in Romania, located in the historical region of Moldavia, and has been one of the leading centers of Romanian social, cultural, academic, and artistic life. In 2018, it was declared the Historical Capital of Romania, noted for its gardens, parks, well-maintained gothic and baroque buildings such as the Theatre and Palace of the Four Museums, and a striking variety of Orthodox churches, each of which has a guide available to give historical commentary.

I went on to the famous monastery of Neamț, where the Staretz (spiritual father) Archimandrite Ephrem hosted me for dinner. We had a five-course meal of vegetables deliciously prepared, with soup, dill pickles, homemade bread, and apple turnovers. After the meal, one of the monks gave me a tour of the monastery, which was constructed in the early-1600s with about sixty monks there at the time of my visit.

From there, I went on to spend a couple of days at the monastery of Sihastria, which means "place of silence." Two of my Romanian Orthodox priest friends in Montreal had suggested I visit Sihastria, as it is the monastery with the strictest observance and the most secluded wilderness setting. There were seventy monks in the community, fifteen of them novices. The iconography adorning the monastery represented the most beautiful harmonizing I'd anywhere seen of Byzantine and Western styles. It's that kind of integration of Eastern with Western elements that makes Romania unique among Orthodox countries.

Br. Stephane took me on a three-hour walk to Sihla Skete, a grotto-shrine cave where St. Theodora, a woman hermit of the late seventeenth to early eighteenth century, once lived. It was a gorgeous trail with frequent vistas of rolling valley and wave after wave of mountains. We climbed steadily for about an hour and a half before arriving at a cave situated in a wild and rugged place. I couldn't find words to explain the feelings and thoughts and movements of the heart occasioned by standing in a place where Theodora became filled with God, divinized. The hagiography says that birds brought bread to her from Sihastria.

A little further away was the skete of Sihla with ten monks. The setting, the buildings, the monks' appearance were so reminiscent of

Mount Athos that I could have sworn I was back on the Holy Mountain in Greece except for one notable difference. On Athos, the response to a Roman Catholic priest is to coolly look him up and down from ten feet away, whereas in Moldavia and Wallachia the monks bow down, take your hand, and kiss it because you are a priest. It makes no difference whether you are Orthodox or Roman Catholic, their response is equally warm and welcoming. Being close to the West geographically, sharing its culture and linguistic heritage, many of them know we in the West are not all corruption and heresy.

HOLY WEEK IN RUSSIA

In April 1985, two of my ecumenical colleagues, the Rev. Dr. Lois Wilson and Anglican Archbishop Michael Peers, led a Canadian ecumenical trip to Russia for Holy Week.

It was an enriching and instructive experience in various ways. As a Christian I am a seeker, and what I seek is an increasingly intense experience of God—an experience inherently limited in a society where sacrifice is to be avoided and service increasingly rendered only for payment. But God carefully chose to be revealed in the "language" of service, for example, in Jesus washing the feet of his disciples, in his dying on the cross. One of the reasons Jesus was not recognized by many as the Messiah was that he came as a suffering servant. In this visit to Russia I was looking for an experience of church where these characteristics of how God is—loving, merciful, and compassionate—were clearly in the forefront. What drew me about Russia is that Christianity is, reportedly, incompatible with "success." To become a regular worshipper is to choose the way of Christ over the way of the world.

The irony is that where I was going (Russia) the ideology is materialism, and the Christians there combat it. Where I was coming from (North America), Christianity is part of the ideology, but materialism is increasingly the practice. Our battle in the West may, strangely enough, be harder to fight precisely because the choices are less clear. Our own Western society espouses materialist, self-aggrandizing principles no less hostile to faith than out-and-out materialism—and this under the banner of some vague theism ("In God we trust"). At least in the Soviet Union the lines were more clearly drawn: materialism was unambiguously identified with atheism. Being a Christian involves an irrevocable break with materialistic, consumer, status-oriented "success."

When our plane arrived in Moscow, the customs agent searched my suitcase and found five copies of *Ecumenism*, the quarterly journal of the Canadian Centre for Ecumenism of which I was the editor. I planned on giving these copies to the Metropolitan and Patriarch of the Russian Orthodox Church. In my backpack, they found four more copies, leftovers from those I had brought along for each member of the group and distributed on the plane. This raised their suspicions as to what I was about in Russia, and they confiscated all but two. They also took the hundred laminated icon cards I had brought to give as gifts to church members there, as well as a Russian copy of the New Testament. When a single copy of *Ecumenism* began to show up in the luggage of our group members, the agents said they wanted them all. So I collected them all and handed them over. It took us two hours to get through customs!

Archimandrite Yelefteri from the Zagorsk monastery was awaiting us as he had been assigned by his community to be a guide for us for our whole two weeks in Russia.

The Baptist Union in Russia has four branches: Evangelicals, Baptists, Pentecostals, and Mennonites. Their 135-year-old motto is "Evangelism, Education, Union." In the year prior to our visit, there were 40,000 new members, and within the previous five years, 262 new congregations. The Baptist community greeted us in Christ's name, gave us a moving concert of music and song, and then broke bread and shared the cup.

On Good Friday morning, we had a tour of the Kremlin and a visit to several churches before participating in the Great Friday Descent from the Cross service at St. Nicholas church. The people were not pretending that they did not know what would happen with this man Jesus who is shown either hanging on the cross or lying in the tomb. All through the service, even on Good Friday, the victory of Christ is proclaimed. This is what the cross with the crucified Lord all decorated with flowers is saying. Even on Good Friday there are "alleluias," and on Easter Sunday, there is the cross. The two are never treated in isolation, one from the other. The tomb at the center of the church was decorated with flowers, and upon it rested a winding cloth with an image of Jesus. It is called in the liturgy "the fountain of our resurrection."

In the West, we tend to be all doom and gloom on Good Friday and all lilies and alleluias on Easter Sunday. To my mind, this reflects more than just a different liturgical tradition. It reflects Christian life in a society where the choices are relatively easy. It's easier to separate the cross from Easter in a society where going to church is cost-free, apart from the few dollars that we might throw into the collection basket. But in a society where being Christian is risky for career-oriented people, where regular churchgoing may mean relinquishing the "ladder of success," choosing to be Christian is not an easy choice and will certainly involve the cross at some point. The "alleluias" will have to be found in the midst of and integrated with the experience of the cross.

I was very glad to have come because it helped me understand something I didn't understand before. Previously, I could see no positive side to life in a persecuted church. But now I see that, paradoxically, there may well be something *easier* about their situation than our own: their choice to be a Christian or not is a clearer one. Being a Christian in North America is in a way more difficult than being a Christian in the former Soviet Union, in the sense that I can call myself a Christian without having to put my job status and respectability on the line. I can live the alleluia and keep the cross largely out of the picture. But is that discipleship? I suspected that these Russian Christians would be somewhat frightened by all our choices and rightfully see in them the potential for a comfortable and compromised Christianity.

As usual, God is confounding the "wisdom of the wise" (i.e., the churches of the West) whose tendency is to look with pity on the plight of the churches in the East. As our guide said to us, "Say what you wish about the compromises the church makes with the state in the Soviet Union. Criticize it if you will. But it is because of these compromises that even these fifty churches in Moscow are open and that the gospel is proclaimed, even if the priests may not be able to preach 'social action' sermons. The people gathered here tonight have heard the unadulterated milk of the gospels passed out upon them for four hours in all its power to infiltrate hearts and minds. They planted their feet and stood with candles lit in rapt attention. I can only guess at how what they heard enlightens their lives."

Chapter 27

AFRICA, NEW ZEALAND, AUSTRALIA, AND INDIA

AFRICA: KENYA AND TANZANIA

In 1988, I went on a church-related study tour to Africa with a group of fifteen participants from various churches. Why go to Africa? Well, because the opportunity to go is a gift of the Spirit inviting one to come more fully alive to the glory and tragedy of this world, to the reality of the human family, to the responsibility each of us has in society, local and worldwide.

What was I looking for? For depth. For inspiration to give my life radically for a cause that stirs my whole being. The unity of the church is an important cause, but do we feel any passion around it? I was feeling less and less interest in talking about structures and church-dividing doctrines, and a growing desire to talk about Jesus. To preach the core message that he has reconciled us to God, and to preach it to those whom he called to be reconciled to one another—his followers in the different churches. The desire to preach the core message of the gospel to divided Christians and give them a prolonged experience of the faith we share was resurfacing in my life with new force, and in my ministry at the Canadian Centre for Ecumenism I had the contacts and base from which to actually do it.

What would the ecumenical benefits be?

- to get people into each other's churches
- to provide people and congregational organizations a chance to get to know one another and look at what they might do together

- to introduce them to another tradition's devotional style
- to give them an experience of shared faith through preaching, prayer, and ritual
- to give them a glimpse of "what could be" in a reunited church of churches
- to confirm them in their covenant, or invite them to consider entering into a covenant
- to be part of a movement of renewal and fresh visioning for all

What I sought was essentially a ministry that would let me carry forward and use my ecumenical experience in doing what I want most to do: talk to people about Jesus, about the Good News of our reconciliation with God, about God's love for us and all that we have to be grateful for.

These are the themes around which I felt energy and passion. I wanted the occasion to share my experience of the risen Lord more personally and directly with people. To do this, I was willing to hit the road, to go to where the people were. The next step of the ecumenical movement, I felt, needs new forms, fresh approaches, and creative initiatives.

NEW ZEALAND, AUSTRALIA, AND INDIA

In the winter of 1991, I went on a five-month study sabbatical to New Zealand, Australia, and India, with the World Council of Churches' every-seven-to-eight-years General Assembly taking place that year in Canberra, Australia, at the heart of it.

Leaving the January ice and snow of winter in Montreal to give some talks and to lead an ecumenical retreat for Anglicans, Catholics, and Presbyterians in the summer season of New Zealand was, to say the least, a pleasurable experience. Following the talks and retreat and prior to going to Australia for the WCC Assembly, I took a week's vacation to explore the vaunted beauty of New Zealand's alps, rugged west coast, and fjords. I've been blessed to see much of the earth's beauty in myriad climates, from seas to mountains to African Serengeti's with their animals wild and free, but the glories of New Zealand brought yelps of incredulity and wonder.

Waterfalls—literally hundreds of them—falling from thousands of feet up, bridal veil falls, rooster-tail falls, all blown by the wind, ribbons of moving-white everywhere slicing up whole loaves of towering granite rock, torrents of water cascading in a festival of aqua!

The South Island seacoast was every bit what I had imagined it to be: wild and breath-taking, profligate with beaches whose vertical cliffs defy access, breakers pounding the rocks, and then the Fox glacier. Never have I been able to get out onto a glacier, peer down into its icy crevasses and turquoise-blue canyons, up at the towers of ice, into the cavernous mouth of the glaciers' terminal point where freezing blue water spews out giant un-melting ice-cubes. It's the incredible variety within a relatively small island that leaves even the veteran traveler astonished.

I engaged in informal worship of the Creator in thanksgiving for the glories of creation, hiking on the glaciers, walking through the rainforests, driving along the rugged seacoast.

AUSTRALIA

The theme of the WCC General Assembly in Auckland was "Come, Holy Spirit, Renew the Whole of Creation." The discussions and debates included ecological problems as well as world disorders: The Gulf War, the weaknesses of the Middle East, the pressure of financial deregulations. Recommendations remained general with respect for international law and the peaceful settlement of conflicts. Part of my responsibility was to provide articles on assembly events for three Canadian national publications as well as for our quarterly periodical *Ecumenism*, which absorbed all my available time and energy in the course of the assembly.

Following the assembly came the opportunity for some sabbatical time in Australia to visit and stay with colleagues in Sydney, Canberra, Alice, and Perth, offering the opportunity to see those cities before going on to India.

INDIA

My subsequent several weeks of sabbatical study in India was devoted to learning more about Eastern religions—Hinduism, Buddhism, and Islam—in their home context. The experience of sitting in on lectures being given by the swamis was one of being introduced into a vast, rich universe of meaning that had evolved slowly over time through the personal experience of wise and dedicated people. They had studied the workings of the mind and senses, the nature of consciousness, in a scientific manner and had deduced methods and techniques in light of their learning to service people's quest for a higher spiritual consciousness.

As a Christian, I knew that methods and techniques have their place. We are incarnate beings and learn through our senses. We don't however generally teach people how to pray, how to meditate, how to develop and cultivate awareness and its relation to God-consciousness. We Christians tend more to give lessons to memorize, books to read, approaches that operate on an intellectual plane but do not necessarily take the mind down into the heart.

In this study tour, the seed was planted in me to write the book *Disciplines for Christian Living: Interfaith Perspectives*,[1] in which chapters are devoted to spiritual practices that can help us put into action what we believe, for example, friendship, marriage, Sabbath, exercise, play, prayer, fasting, and service. Together they form a holistic composite, taking into account the physical, affective, intellectual, and spiritual dimensions of our lives. A dream began to form in my mind of a Christian center for spiritual development. It would be a place of instruction in disciplines, methods, and techniques for westerners in their spiritual journey. That dream took form three years later in the Unitas center for spirituality and Christian meditation in Montreal.

Ten years earlier in 1980–81, I had spent a study semester of the different Christian traditions at the Bossey Ecumenical Institute in Switzerland. Now, a decade later, I was spending a study sabbatical among Hindus, Buddhists, and Muslims, from which study I would return more self-consciously Christian than I had ever been! When one grows up in the West, Christianity is part of the woodwork, and because it is represented by churches all around town, one doesn't derive a sense of its specialness.

The curious mind, however, runs farther afield, looks across the fence at more exotic pastures and more easily finds something to interest it there because we are always enticed by the strange and the new. But after entering into those pastures and grazing there awhile, one is better qualified to evaluate and appreciate the "quality of the grass" where one was born and raised. It is only by crossing-over and grazing in Hinduism and Buddhism and Islam that I came to appreciate more deeply the distinctive taste, texture, and nutritional value of Christianity.

That which the Hindu and Buddhist strive for with all their might—the state of freedom from cyclic rebirth and suffering—the Christian joyfully accepts in Christ's trampling down suffering by suffering and death by death, bringing us freedom and life as a gift from God. As our scriptures tell us, we were made for love, for communion of life with God, loving God with our whole heart, our whole mind, our whole soul, and with all our strength, and our calling is to love our neighbor as ourselves. Any teaching that stops short of this fundamental truth of our existence yet needs fulfillment and enlightenment.

A keystone experience for me of my time in India was a month at the Shanthivanam ashram in South India. Shanthivanam is an Indian Christian Ashram belonging to the Camaldolese congregation of the Order of Saint Benedict (O.S.B.Cam.). The Ashram was founded in 1950 by Fr. Jules Monchanin and Fr. Henri Le Saux from France, and then established by Fr. Bede Griffiths from England. It was their vision to acculturate western monasticism with Indian asceticism. They were greatly impressed with the spirituality of the Eastern religions such as Hinduism, Buddhism, Islamism, Taoism, and the traditions and culture on which they were based.

In order to establish this thought process, they ventured to raise the Sacchidanada Ashram as a pioneering attempt at Indian Christian Ashrams. The aim of the Ashram was to initiate a way of contemplative life based on the traditions of Christian monasticism and of Hindu spiritual commitment and practice. The Christian devotee's life at the ashram is thus based both on the *Rule of St. Benedict*, the patriarch of western monasticism on the teachings of the monastic fathers of the church rooted in Catholicism, and in the study of Hindu doctrine making use of Indian ways of prayer and meditation. Not surprisingly, it was during my time at this ashram that I was introduced to yoga, which gradually took root as a component in my meditation practice.

The Second Vatican Council, in its declaration *Nostra Aetate* on "Non-Christian Religions," said that the church rejects nothing that is true and holy in these religions and encouraged Catholics to recognize, preserve, and promote the spiritual and moral values as well as the social and cultural values to be found among them.

I was given a little cabin at the ashram, close to a nearby river and surrounded by eucalyptus and palm trees, and daily joined the community in their chapel for daily prayer, the Eucharist, and meditation. The quiet time in-between was appreciably used for spiritual reading, writing, and reflection.

After a month of retreat at Shantivanam, I took a ten-day course in Buddhism at the Tushita Centre in Dharamsala. I appreciated its teachings on nonattachment; its encouragement for mindfulness, which has become a societal theme in our North American culture today; its reminder that all things are ultimately fleeting; its high code of ethics and personal responsibility; its spiritual discipline of meditation for purifying the mind; its compassion for all living beings; and its commitment to nonviolence—all of which gave me a perspective of Buddhism as more of a psychology than a religion.

For it tells me nothing of my Creator, Redeemer, and Sanctifier, in whose love for humankind God became one of us and freely gave his life in love for us, dwelling within our very hearts and setting us free from the burden of sin and guilt, free to serve in loving gratitude all our days. But while it doesn't worship God, Buddhism is more of a psychology that works toward a clear, calm, positive state of mind through the avoidance of greed, anger, jealousy, and the like.

I also took a course in Hinduism that left me grateful for the rich tradition of spiritual wisdom contained in the Vedenta; the deep insight contained in the Upanishads into the nature of God as one. The call in the Bhagavad Gita to do my duty, to do what is right, entering into the din of daily battles but keeping my heart peaceful by not being attached from the results of my efforts, leaving results to God. There is a remarkable resonance with Christian trinitarian perspectives in Hinduism's conviction of God's transcendence in Brahman and God's immanence and presence to one's personal self in Atman. I was also grateful for the rich devotional life and faith of the people who are ready to recognize "The Formless One" manifested in any form and present in all things; grateful for the holy lives of sannyasis and sadhus/wandering ascetics; grateful for the carefully researched and refined science of yoga as a way of calming the mind and body and preparing one for contemplation. But in the end, Hinduism leaves me imprisoned in circular thinking, karmic rebirth, and the caste system. It tells me I must get out of this on my own or eternally come 'round, strapped to the wheel of karma, paying for my weakness, ignorance, and sinfulness with repeated reincarnations. Never before had the Easter refrain sung repeatedly by Orthodox Christians in the Easter season sounded in my heart with greater rejoicing: "Trampling down death by death, and suffering by suffering, Christ brings freedom and life to those who are in the tomb." The Christian *lives* in nirvana—the state of freedom from cyclic rebirth and suffering. That which the Hindu and Buddhist strives for with all their might, the Christian joyfully accepts as a free gift of God.

I went to North India to visit retreat centers in Varanasi, Agra, Delhi, Hardwar, and Dharmsala for a personal experience of their offerings in the domain of spirituality. In the course of my experiences, a dream began to take shape within me of initiating, once back home, a center for spiritual development that would teach westerners disciplines, methods, and techniques for their spiritual journey. The form that dream eventually took was Unitas.

BACK TO AUSTRALIA

After spending March, April, and May in India, I returned to Australia, devoting most of the month of June to giving twenty-seven talks over twenty-four days in the various cities and churches around this island nation, talks covering a wide range of topics, for example, Ecumenical Spirituality, Christian Meditation, Spirituality and Sports, and Family Life.

In "coming up for air" and looking for something fun to do, I gambled and won in deciding to take a boat over to Rotts Nest Island, eleven kilometers off the coast and had a delightful day there biking around the island. It was so peaceful! No motor-driven vehicles, just cyclists on good roads with constantly changing seascapes to delight the eye. Beaches upon beaches, secluded, deserted. Dunes and promontories. Royal blue water. How dramatic a contrast from the crowded roads, honking horns, polluted air, and dense populations of India.

For a week, I stayed with Peter Wiltshire, a Uniting Church minister and Australian Christian meditation network coordinator. Peter had arranged for three members of a monastic community forty-five minutes from Melbourne in Geelong to come to his house for lunch: Graham, a Baptist; Steve, an Anglican, both spiritual fathers to the monastic community; and Cheryl. In our several-hours conversation I was delighted to discover an ecumenical monastic community emanating largely from members of free church traditions.

Their community is one of the amazing expressions of the emergence of a new reality in the church—an ecumenical monastic tradition. When I visited its chapel, I saw icons, a tabernacle with reserved Eucharist, a recessed baptismal pool in the form of a cross, and a spirituality that celebrates thematically the life of Christ across the days of each week. Monday: Birth, Tuesday: Baptism, Wednesday: Transfiguration, Thursday: Eucharist, Friday: Death, Saturday: Descent, and Sunday: Resurrection.

Initiated around 1970, the Community of the Transfiguration[2] is composed of women and men, married and celibate, with houses on the same street in commonly owned property in regular neighborhoods of Australian towns. Their values include the promotion of the separation of church and state, the championing of human rights and dignity, and the importance of a personal relationship with God. The Community has also eagerly embraced ecumenism and has drawn on both Catholic and Orthodox models to deepen their communal and spiritual lives. Proof positive of a new phenomenon: ecumenically minded people from different churches who feel more in common with each other than with non-ecumenically minded members of their own church.

The Community/Monastery has retained its Baptist identity and yet is not like any other Baptist community. Its life and structure are shaped both by the historical legacy of monasticism and the reconfiguration of that legacy by new monasticism. Community members believe they are called to replant and nurture monastic life in the midst of an exploitative, consumer-oriented, individualistic society. By their observance of monastic practices such as obedience and stability and the common purse, they seek to live lives that are congruent with their community rule such as gratitude, love, prayer, and truth-telling. They seek to manifest "the same mind as was in Christ Jesus."

Offering radical love, Community members challenge the domination and reign of evil, first within their own hearts and then in the world. They avoid activism for its own sake, seeking instead to be conformed to God's image through protest and solidarity on issues ranging from workers' rights to the treatment of refugees.

But this activity is ultimately resourced and enabled by the spiritual discipline of the Community, by the daily round of prayer that seeks always to orient works toward the loving will of God.

After our visit to the monastery, Peter and his wife took me to a wildlife sanctuary where great care is being taken to preserve the unique national heritage of animals in Australia. We had a delightful time scratching the wombat's tummy, stroking the kangaroos and wallabies, and watching the strange platypus and echidna, both egg-laying mammals. The real treasure of this Australian visit was staying with couples and families and religious communities in each place. This gave me a glimpse into the "real" Australia.

Sydney was more of a "turn-on" than either Perth or Melbourne or Canberra from a sight-seeing point of view. It struck me as the most beautiful modern city I had seen anywhere in the world. Bright and clean, with so many visually stimulating vistas and enough interesting and fun things to do to occupy a full-time tourist for a week. It's a really impressive city, and I managed to get to see a good part of it in the time I had.

I also went down to the beach and walked, allowing all the events enjoyed there to flicker slowly past the light of memory, reexperiencing each place and the people and events. Then I just laid down on my towel on the sand with all that fullness and listened to the waves and watched the clouds. The joy of being!

The following morning, I thought that I would expire of bliss. I got up to watch the sun rise out of the sea and then went for a jog along the hard, flat beach at the water's edge. Finally, in the warming light of the early morning sun, I dove in the placid warm water for a sublimely delicious swim! They call this "winter" in Australia.

My visit to each of the cities was a fair balance of work and play, "on" and "off" time.

Chapter 28

IRELAND, IONA, SOUTH AFRICA, ENGLAND, AND SWITZERLAND

LEAVING MONTREAL AND UNITAS FOR NEW YORK CITY

In 1999, after twenty-two years of various ministries in Montreal, the Paulist leadership was calling me back to the United States. "We like the ministry you're engaged in there, and we'd like to call you to return to the States and open and develop the ministry of a Paulist National Office for Ecumenical and Interfaith Relations here." Well, I knew there would surely be people and things I would miss—our mixed community at Unitas, French, Mount Royal, a daily schedule built around two meditation periods, my lovely room and balcony, the garden. The whole living situation at Unitas was a gift. Now there was an opportunity to practice enjoying the gifts given.

My ministry in ecumenism has been particularly blessed with people and intercultural experiences. When I look back on my life, I am overwhelmed by its rich and colorful texture. I see now how the move to New York City was divinely guided, and how that move, like all the other evolutionary developments in my ministerial life, catapulted me into a new and larger orbit, just as everything that had gone before me at the Canadian Centre for Ecumenism prepared me for Unitas.

IRELAND AND IONA

Within my first year back in the United States in 1999, I was invited to lead a retreat on the island of Iona that sits off the west coast of the Isle of Mull in the historic Highlands of Scotland. St. Columba came there in 563 to establish an abbey that still stands. The island is known as the birthplace of Celtic Christianity in Scotland.

A remarkable aspect of the trip was all the natural beauty I was able to see: Achill Island, cliffs and the sea. Aran Islands. Skellig Michael. The Dingle and Iveragh peninsulas. A train ride through the Scottish Highlands and a ferry through the inner Hebrides. My soul was immensely fed and enriched by all these experiences. For the first time, I felt like I understood something of the history of my ancestors. Having some time there was an appreciable learning experience.

A few years later (2003), when I came to lying in bed one night, my sense was that I didn't have any plans to revise or dreams unrealized. I was doing exactly what I longed to do—leading retreats, preaching missions on themes that touch life's core meaning, offering courses and programs in our vibrant New York City parish. In my free time, there were opportunities to travel to places I wanted to experience: Ireland, Scotland, Crete, and China. "If I were to be told I had just a year to live, I would just keep on doing what I'm doing because I love it, and all I have to say to you, Lord, is Thank you!"

When I got up in the morning, I spent some time reflecting on the spirituality of travel.

SPIRITUALITY OF TRAVEL

Virtues required: patience, flexibility, detachment, acceptance of dependency.

WHAT YOU HAVE TO LET GO OF AND HAVE LITTLE-TO-NO CONTROL OVER WHEN YOU TRAVEL:

1. The heat in the house
2. The food in the refrigerator, on the shelf, and on the table
3. The mattress you sleep on

4. Convenient nighttime access to a bathroom when you may want it
5. A place to workout
6. Knowledge of how to get from one place to another
7. Ability to get online and access email

BUT WHAT A GREAT SCHOOL IN THE SPIRITUAL LIFE TRAVEL IS! IT TEACHES ME ABOUT:

1. Traveling light
2. Cultivating new tastes
3. Living from a sense of the giftedness of everything
4. The importance of a routine of daily prayer that grounds the flux of the day
5. The value in diversity (liturgical/musical styles; menus)
6. Getting along with people as an essential value in living
7. The particular gifts and virtues of different confreres
8. The illusion of autonomy
9. Being at ease with the fact of my life that I depend on God and others for everything

I liked living in this neighborhood of New York City very much. Having a parish in which I could minister as a priest was wonderful and proved to be a good source of friendships. My office quarters were ideal. Also there in the city were the network of offices it made most sense for me to be working with.

In terms of the work the community was asking me to do, I personally believed that the decision we made in 1999 to locate this office in New York City was a good one and that this was the best place for me to advance the work. But signals were now emerging that I might soon be asked to move the office to Washington, DC. The decision, it seemed, would go in that direction by the sheer pull of the community leadership's need to legitimate all the money being invested in renovations of St. Paul's College and the creation of a Hecker Center for Ministry in Washington, DC, that would house the Paulist community's national ministries. I was, however, confident that, should all that come to pass, there would also be new networks, new advantages I would discover, new friendships, and new opportunities for ministry there as had been the case in New York City.

SOUTH AFRICA

The Parliament of the World's Religions was taking place in Cape Town, South Africa, in December 1999. A few friends and I decided to go over early to see some of the surrounding terrain in Botswana and Namibia as well as in South Africa. Our first visit was to Wetlands National Park. We took a three-hour boat ride up and down the river, seeing hippopotamuses, crocodiles, heron, term, and kingfishers.

The following day we went to Hluhluwe-Imfolozi Game Reserve Park, the oldest nature reserve in Africa, 690 kilometers of hilly topography known for its rich wildlife and conservation efforts. We were not disappointed! We saw leopards, rhinos, giraffes, Cape buffaloes, zebras, and hundreds of antelopes. What a plunge into the reality of Africa! The next morning, I took a hike in the park with a ranger. For two and a half hours, we hiked up and down hills, along the riverbeds, and through the tall grass reserve, knowing that it was just us (and his gun!) and the animals. We saw scads of wildlife, unnervingly close up. Zebras, rhinos, Cape buffalo, giraffe, and so close to impalas we could practically touch them if we wanted to.

When my friends and I got back in the car later that day, two rhinos walked across the road right in front of us and stood alongside it. The friend driving said, "Should I pass or just sit here?" To which the other responded, "Go ahead. The car's insured on our visa card."

We proceeded to drive northwest through the stunningly beautiful countryside of Swaziland, emerald-green mountain valleys, mountain ridges all around, and visited the Swazi Cultural Centre, enjoying the singing and dancing there, as well as a commentated tour by a Swazi native in and around twenty-two thatched huts.

The following day we saw the "king of the jungle"—lions—eight of them! The first two were lying across the roadside lake, but clearly discernible. The next pair, male and female, were lying together about fifteen yards from the road. We tried to get them to stand up and move around a bit, but no luck. Then, about an hour later, we rounded a corner and were met by four female lions who walked nonchalantly right at us, before turning and strolling into the brush. Not long after that, we saw our first elephant, who also came at the car before we slowly proceeded and passed by. Several other firsts in the day: ringed waterbuck, ostriches, hyenas, velvet monkeys, baboons, hippos, giraffes, wildebeests, impalas. It was, to say the least, exciting!

We also enjoyed our overnights in the park facilities that offered a variety of accommodations—tent, trailer, hut, chalet. But there was no place where you could hike or walk in these game parks. The best one could do was to walk around the fenced-in perimeter of the campground a few times. We were ready to leave the animals to their wilds and see some of the rest of South Africa. Among our visits were the monuments and museums in Praetoria and Johannesburg. On American Thanksgiving Day, we gave thanks for faith, health, education, the opportunities to learn and marvel at the diversity of God's creation in all its people and cultures, animals and architecture, flora and fauna!

Then we went on to a long day's drive through the arid desert of Botswana, traveling the following day to Keetmanshoop in Namibia. We were drawn to overnight at a place five kilometers out of a town that had a big sign "Welcome to Texas" over the gate, and cabins named after New Orleans, Santa Fe, Colorado, and so on. All toilets were marked "Cowboys" or "Cowgirls," and there was a Western-style bar with country music. Not what one would expect in Africa! The next morning we went into town for church. The liturgy lasted an hour and a half with everything sung. The preacher's homily was on the "A-B-C's of Aids prevention." A-Abstinence. B-Be faithful to your partner. C-Condomize. Or D-Die.

Africa was certainly not expensive. We were able to live comfortably on a budget of $25–30 a day for food and lodging. From Namibia, we headed south to Cape Town for the World Parliament of Religions in South Africa.

THE WORLD PARLIAMENT OF RELIGIONS

The 1999 Parliament of the World's Religions was held December 1–8 in Cape Town, South Africa. Over 7,000 people from around the world—teachers, scholars, leaders, believers, practitioners—came together to experience the spiritual and cultural variety, to exchange insights, to share wisdom, and to celebrate their unique religious identities. In short, to be amazed, delighted, and inspired.

In the program, participants dealt with the critical issues facing the global community, becoming more informed about the world situation, and seeking the moral and ethical convergence that leads to shared commitment and action. It was also a memorable testimony to the good hearts and goodwill of people from every part of the world and from almost every religious and spiritual tradition. They joined with one another in a spirit of dialogue and cooperation, seeking to discover new ways to rise to the challenges and the opportunities of life at the threshold of a new century.

Here are a few highlights just to give you a taste of what the Parliament is like. The opening evening was enlivening with an awesome drumming exhibition by thirteen Japanese in an open-air amphitheater and Hindu classical dance, followed by a talk on "The Interfaith Movement; Where We Are Now, and Where We're Going," by a professor at St. Francis' College in Queens, New York. The following morning, there was another talk ("Can We Pray Together?") by a professor at Drew University in New Jersey just forty minutes from Manhattan where I lived—two great back-home contacts for me to make.

Other talk themes in the course of the Parliament:

"Spirituality: The Heart of Islam"
"Toward an Understanding of Abrahamic Faiths"
"Grassroots Interfaith Dialogue: Connecting at the Heart Level"
"The Mystic Heart"
"Applying Buddhist Values in Building a Culture of Peace"
"Tools for Interfaith Dialogue"

Another evening plenary gave a cultural sense of the place of ritual in our lives with a woman doing Tai Chi to a classical rendition of the Prayer of St. Francis, and an African choir, Indian classical dancers, and a pop singer offering "Be the Vision, Be the Dream." I felt a deep sense of appreciation for the human family in all its richness.

Nelson Mandela was the plenary speaker on one of the evenings. I led two workshops that generated some good questions, discussion, and sharing among participants as people brought their own experience. A few South Africans offered to show me the Cape Town area, which I very much appreciated seeing. In the days following the Parliament, my pre-Parliament colleagues and I had a fabulous day trip down to Cape Point and Cape of Good Hope, which offered the most stunning seascapes I'd seen anywhere—South Island, New Zealand, and Newfoundland, Canada, included! The turquoise color of the sea reminded me of Greece. The drive over Chapman's Peak down into Hout's Bay was one of the most breathtaking drives I have ever taken. It was a wonderful way to end the journey!

CHALLENGE AND PROMISE

The challenge and promise of "mission ministry" is to learn to live interculturally. In short, it gives one the opportunity to learn from and live with people from different cultural backgrounds.

On a Poustinia day in September 2008, I was reflecting on my life and how the invitations, the ministry, seemed to be intensifying. I had crossed the country three times that summer: I was in San Francisco in June; on Vancouver Island in August; and in Alaska and Arizona in September. There had been an itinerant dimension to my ministry since 1980, but I had never been this on-the-go. What was happening? Was it just that my ecumenical and interfaith ministry was coming to maturation? Gaining notoriety? Or was it that there were fewer and fewer of us doing the work? Or did it simply witness to my several irons in the fire, for example, Christian unity, interreligious relations, spirituality, and yoga?

An email from our seminary director Steve Bossi arrived, trying to set up a formation program for our students in the fall on Sunday afternoons from the end of September through the beginning of December. "How many and which Sunday afternoons could you give?" he wanted to know. I looked at my calendar and responded, "Just one." I was scheduled on all the rest of them, and those are *Sundays*!

Then that morning another email came in. It was an invitation from a Swami in an ashram on Paradise Island in the Bahamas asking me to come and to teach about Catholicism, the mission of the Paulists, and interfaith relations in a big conference he was running December 22, 2008, to January 1, 2009. Two days after that, an invitation arrived asking me to come back to Phoenix in January 2009 to lead a weekend meditation retreat on the Role of Prayer in the Work for Christian Unity.

What I saw as I looked to the year ahead was a marked increase in more formal ecumenical and interfaith engagements—the

Jewish-Christian dialogue group in DC; a summer course to teach at Fordham University in New York City; formation talks to Paulist novices and training sessions for students; invitations to light-fires-in-others for the work for Christian unity, coming from Minnesota (St. Cloud diocesan clergy), Arizona (church leaders retreat), and two workshops on interfaith prayer at the National Workshop on Christian Unity.

These were all "bullseyes" to what was at the heart of my office's mission statement. I was anticipating invitations coming from the National Council of Churches to represent the Paulists in the work of the Faith and Order commission; from John Borelli to participate in the Rumi-Georgetown University dialogue; and from James Masa at the Bishops' Conference Ecumenical and Interfaith Affairs office to take on some work. It was going to be a *huge* year in terms of work, and it made me nervous just looking at the calendar. It would require me to be extremely grounded in my daily disciplines of prayer and exercise; my weekly pillars of Sabbath rhythm, fast day, and eve with friends; my monthly practice of a Poustinia day.

IRELAND, ENGLAND, AND SWITZERLAND

In 2010, my Paulist confrere Tom Kane and I led a special study-pilgrimage for about twenty-five people in which we visited various reconciliation and ecumenical/interfaith centers in Europe. Our aspiration was to experience different models of reconciliation and interfaith ministry as a way to stimulate our approaches to related ministries in North America. We had meetings with key leaders in each area with specially designed prayer services and liturgies. In Northern Ireland we visited the cities of Belfast and Derry to meet with religious leaders to explore the troubled history and traditions of Northern Ireland. We also stayed in a lovely hotel along the seacoast, visited the North Antrim Coast, and spent a day at the Corrymeela Community in Ballycastle, which has been in the forefront of ecumenical peacemaking.

In London, England, we had time to explore this world capital, to meet with leaders at St. Ethelburga's Interfaith Reconciliation Centre, and to spend a day at the Coventry Cathedral where we learned about the ongoing commitment to reconciliation on the part of the Cathedral community after it was bombed during World War II.

In Geneva, Switzerland, we explored this historic city 500 years after John Calvin's tenure and visited the headquarters of the World Council of Churches, learning more about its ongoing ecumenical and interfaith work. We also met with interreligious leaders in the canton of Geneva. We concluded our pilgrimage with a festive dinner against the background of the Alps on Lake Geneva.

Chapter 29

THE CARIBBEAN, INDIA, AND NEPAL

In 2012, I served as a Holy Week chaplain on a cruise ship to the Caribbean islands of Puerto Rico, Dominica, Barbados, and Antigua. I had never been to any of these islands. Our first stop was Puerto Rico, where we spent a full day in the old city. We had a great day in San Juan, very picturesque with narrow streets and many shops featuring Puerto Rican art. We hit the streets in old town by 9:00 a.m. and took in the sights until about 4:00 p.m. The Church of San Francesco and the Cultural Museum of Puerto Rico were highlights. I was amazed to learn that the native people—"Archaic Indians" from the northern part of South America—go back to the fourth century BC.

On Palm Sunday I participated in the palm procession from San Giuseppe Church to the Cathedral. They had a whole group of young adults dressed in the robes of Jesus's time, walking behind the bishop, with a full reading of the passion of Christ in the cathedral church.

The island of Tortola was also a worthwhile outing and the hike through "the caves and baths" was the stuff of J.R.R. Tolkien. This unusual geological formation consists of massive, time-smoothed boulders piled up in stacks and clusters, which naturally creates intimate grottos, stunning beaches and oasis-like pools between them. One can enjoy spectacular trails, rejuvenate in secluded pools, explore dazzling grottos, swim, sun, and relax on the beach in this resplendent destination. I delighted in a half-hour swim in the sea, enjoying the coral and occasional fish below, as well as a trek through the caves and baths.

The island of Antigua was once Britain's primary military base in the Caribbean in the 1780s. It has 365 beaches, and in 2009 renamed its highest mountain peak Obama. Once back on the ship, we went on to Dominica, which was named by Christopher Columbus in 1493. This island is twenty-six million years old and is the wildest of all the Caribbean islands. It's known as the "nature island" of the Caribbean and is fiercely committed to ecological preservation, winning awards for eco-tourism. I got off the ship and within five minutes was on a trail to visit the rainforest, waterfalls, botanical gardens, and mountainous vistas along the way.

One night as I was returning to my room following our onboard Holy Thursday service for Holy Week, I ran into a rabbi and his wife. We stopped and visited, and he invited me to their Passover service and their Seder supper the following evening. It was a wonderful opportunity to refresh my memory of the Seder prayers as well as enjoy conversation with them over supper after the service.

The following day was one of the most literally prayer-full Good Fridays I have ever lived. After my morning meditation, I just immersed myself in preparation for the liturgy, then headed off for three quiet, reflective, prayerful hours on the beach. Then it was back to the boat for another dry run of the liturgy, preparing to celebrate it with an onboard overflow gathering of fellow believers. After our Good Friday service, I entered into the three-hour Passover Seder prayer service and meal experience with Jews. It was a memorable day.

On Saturday evening, we had a wonderful Easter Vigil celebration, with singing and music throughout. It was an upbeat and energizing celebration of Jesus's resurrection. People clapped at the end and went out singing the alleluia.

I really enjoyed having a pastoral ministry during this Holy Week and having a group of people to whom to minister. I also learned a good deal about the history of the islands we visited. I didn't even know the names of most of them before. The guides on our island excursions were very good and gave me a feel for the life of the people on the island today. I like to open myself to new experiences, learn new things, and see parts of the world I've never visited. Our tour of these islands was a marvelous experience, ministerially, educationally, and recreationally.

INDIA AND NEPAL

In 2015, my Paulist classmate Tomaso Kane and I led another trip. It was a special interfaith and intercultural study-pilgrimage of twenty-five people to India and Nepal to visit temples, learn of various spiritual traditions, and see the intercultural mix of Christianity with different world religions. It was a pilgrimage designed for both spiritual seekers interested in learning more about different spiritual practices and the religiously committed interested in the potential for mutual enrichment in the interreligious encounter.

We began in Delhi where we explored India's largest mosque, and then enjoyed a rickshaw tour through the bustling urban area before going on to what's called the "Pink City" of Jaipur where, riding on elephants, we visited the Amber Fort and many Hindu temples. We then headed to the formal royal city of Fatehpur Sikri, one of the finest examples of Mughal architecture, before heading the next day to the Taj Mahal, one of the world's most famous architectural monuments.

Then we flew to Varanasi on the Ganges, considered the holiest city of India, and visited the Kashi Vishwanath Temple, which stands on the western bank of the river Ganges and is one of the most revered temples dedicated to Shiva.

From there we went on to Sarnath, where Gautama Buddha gave his first sermon after attaining enlightenment. Sarnath is also a religious and sacred place for Jains. We witnessed the thousand-year-old Aarti ceremony during which worshippers pray near the water in the evening by the light of candles and lanterns. The following morning at sunrise, we took a boat ride on the Ganges, full of pilgrims doing their morning water rituals in the river.

We then traveled to Chennai where we celebrated the liturgy at Saint Thomas Cathedral, a Roman Catholic basilica built in the sixteenth century by Portuguese explorers over the tomb of St. Thomas the apostle. From there, we visited Mylapore on the seacoast, the place of the martyrdom of St. Thomas, as well as an Eastern Rite Catholic Community in the area. Then we drove along the seashore to Mahabalipuram, an ancient seaside town where there are sculptural marvels—shrines and huge sculptures cut out of rocks more than 1,200 years ago, examples of Dravidian-style of architecture. Our next travel site was Pondicherry, a former French colony on the east coast of South India, and from there we were on to Tanjore, a city of temples.

We then headed toward Shantivanam Ashram, where I had made a month's retreat in my first visit to India in 1991. It was founded in 1950 by Fr. Jules Monchanin and Dom Henry LeSaux, the pioneers of Indian-Christian dialogue. They entrusted the ashram community and its work to Dom Bede Griffiths. The Ashram, a center of contemplative life and dialogue between Christianity and Hinduism, was the perfect place for our final days. Its peace and quietude provided us with a supportive environment to review and process together the experiences lived as we concluded our pilgrimage.

A number of changes had taken place in the ashram since my time there twenty-four years earlier, but it was powerful for me to be back in the place where the Lord had planted the seeds for a whole new development in my life—writing the *Prayer of Heart and Body*; becoming a yoga instructor; starting what has become an international network of Christian teachers of yoga; and the christianspracticingyoga.com website now accessed around the world.

My first experience with yoga and the opportunity to practice it linked to meditation happened in this ashram. The Spirit fertilized and watered the seeds and they bore fruit for the service of the people of God at a time when yoga was beginning to go mainstream back in North America, but where there were very few Christians making any effort to help all those of Christian background engaging with yoga to do so in a way coherent with their own faith.

It was moving for me as well to sit in the hut of Fr. Bede, now deceased, remembering his tutelage and leadership, and to find the hut that I'd stayed in, and look out again from it at the eucalyptus trees in the forest. The chapel services happily had the same bhajan chants, rhythm, and music. Our time there was just a few days, but it was enough to fill me with a sense of gratitude and amazement at the surprising things God can do with our lives when we simply say, "Use me, Lord."

THE STRESSES OF TRAVEL

When we got back home, it wasn't long before I had four tightly scheduled events in my calendar: a Gospel Call parish mission; an event in Vermont from Sunday to Wednesday; a day at the Providence Centre, Rhode Island, on "The Mystics"; a weekend in Westfield, Massachusetts, on "Challenge and Inspiration from other Churches and other Religions," and talks the following day with teachers in Montreal, and as they drew near, two were canceled due to weather.

What a delight it was to have a few days in the week ahead to just now sit quietly and serenely work away, ticking off one thing after another from the sizable to-do list. What a blessing those two canceled events were! It would have been an extremely stressful workweek trying to pull everything together in time. Instead, it was productive without stress.

My prayer was, "Please, Lord, help me learn from this experience to avoid boxing myself in in the future with tightly scheduled engagements that leave inadequate time in between them for the preparation required!" The situation that sets it up is classically like this: you get one primary invitation, and then others in the area try to piggyback something onto that, knowing they won't have to pay for the transportation. When you are ten months away from it all, you say, "Sure." Then, as the time draws near, you say to yourself, "What was I thinking?" So, please, Lord, help me to say, "No, I'm sorry, but it's too tightly scheduled and I'm not going to do that to myself anymore."

Chapter 30

WE ARE NOT ALONE ON OUR JOURNEY

THE SWISS ALPS

In 2015, I was enjoying the glories of the Swiss Alps in the mountain chalet of a Swiss friend. It was a spectacular June day without a cloud in the sky and the temp was about 68 degrees Fahrenheit. I just felt like I was in a fantasyland.

One of the nearby trails is a long—and in some places quite steep—ascent to the peak of Mount Tsaté. I decided to hike up to the peak, and the experience of the hike was an occasion for me to recognize that I was getting older! I knew there was a time when I would have been able to just march on up with a steady pace, but that time was past. I had been at the chalet for five days at that point, so I figured that my respiratory system should be adjusted to the altitude...but I was having to stop and just *breathe* every couple of minutes. In the end, I hiked up to Tsaté alpage (cow meadows), but not up to Col de Tsaté, the peak.

The streams running down the mountains were big and fast. At the point on the trail where you leave the gravel road, cross a stream, and then start hiking up a steep path, the stream had about four branches to it, making crossing the stream very challenging. I kept climbing until I found a place where the soaked and grassy soil between each of the stream's branches were close enough to be able to leap over.

Once across, I started climbing up the path again and along the way reached for my water bottle to take a drink. But it wasn't there!

Oh, my gosh, I thought, it must have been thrown out of my waist belt bottle holder on one of my leaps or near falls! Given that it was a bottle my friend had lent me and the only one in the chalet that fit into my fanny pack bottle holder, I decided to go back down and look for it, recognizing that it likely fell into the roaring stream and just got carried down the mountain. When I scanned the place of my crossing, I did not see it anywhere. I figured that I could make the rest of the hike without water, so started climbing again.

Once in the alpage, I saw there was an option of going down a longer but different way and was tempted to do it. But as I hadn't seen another person on the trail coming up behind me, I decided to take the shorter route back and have a chance to keep an eye out for the lost Klean Kanteen.

"Jesus," I prayed, "I know anything is possible with you." So down I went, and when I came to the place where I had made my leaps across the branches of flowing streams, in my leap now between the second and third stream branches, my forward momentum and the wet, soft, grassy soil on which I landed brought me reeling forward onto all fours. I took a deep breath, grateful I had made it, and I opened my eyes to see a deep hole right between my knees, and there, down in the hole, lay the Klean Kanteen! I cried out, "O my God!" Then I added, "Jesus, I knew you could do it! I feel your love. I see your smile."

A coincidence like this—that I would fall right above the lost-and-sought object that, given that it had fallen into a hole, would not have been otherwise visible—is a classic example of the saying, "A coincidence is a little miracle in which God wishes to remain anonymous." It was definitely for me a sign of your presence with me, Lord! We are not alone on our journey!

One year later in 2016, after I moved to Boston, I had a similar experience. A short time after my arrival, I had marked a few days off in my calendar to explore my new home city and get to know better where things are in it. So, I hopped on my bike one Saturday at 8:30 a.m. and headed down to South Boston on the Green Bike Trail. When I got down to the end of Summer Street and came out on Carson Beach, I was blown away! I didn't even know there was access to an ocean beach in Boston, and it's huge! The paved beach walkway all around to the right led me to the John F. Kennedy Museum, which was also on my list to go and visit.

I then went out to Castle Island, which I'd heard people refer to but had no idea where it was. Another beautiful park, to say nothing of the historic fort—William III, named after King William, which served as the fort for the British garrison from 1700 until the revolution in 1776, after which Samuel Adams renamed it Fort Independence. From Castle Island, I biked along the South Boston harbor. It was all in all a fabulous three-hour outing.

A highlight of the day was a guardian angel experience. On the Carson beach right-side point, I took my bike map out from the carrier behind my seat and tucked it under the belt of my fanny pack over my stomach where it would be easy to take out and consult. About twenty minutes later after I'd biked a distance beyond the JFK Museum, I stopped to check my map to see how far the trail extended—only to discover that, unbeknownst to me, the map had fallen out of my belt. Bummer, as this whole area was new to me! Given that this had happened right on the seashore where there's a steady wind, it was now probably a good distance off the trail in the brush to one side or into the water on the other.

Nonetheless, I prayed to my guardian angel to help me find it, turned around, and began backtracking the route I'd traveled since inserting the map under my belt, looking about as I rode along. But when I reached the point where I had put it in my belt, I gave up hope of finding it and just continued on my way. A few minutes later as I rode along, I saw a colorful folded sheet lying flat on the paved trail. I looked back at it as I passed it and thought, "Could that be my map?" Then I turned around and went back to look more closely at it, and it *was* my map! It was one of those mystical moments where I felt my guardian angel's presence and big smile. It could have been blown further away in the wind or been picked up by another walker or rider on the trail...but there it was!

CLOSING

I can only look back in amazement at where you have led me, Lord, the experiences you have given me to live, the places you have sent me. That "Year of Blessing," for example, in 1980–81. Or the three months in New Zealand, Australia, and India. Then the three months between Unitas and coming to New York City during which I made a forty-day Ignatian retreat; went to South Africa for the Parliament of World Religions; and traveled through Swaziland,

Botswana, and Namibia before coming back. All those experiences helped me in personally deepening the themes of the spiritual life and in sharing on these subjects with others.

The older I get, the more deeply I identify with Paul the apostle and John of the Cross. Their lives speak to me on various levels: their constant travel in taking the gospel out to others; the central place in their teachings and writings of the mystery of Christ's indwelling presence; the many balls-in-air that each one had going. I can relate to it all.

Over the years, I've become more aware of how my itinerant lifestyle was making its own positive contribution to my awareness of the Lord's presence with me every step along the way. Over time it helped me to journey light with only the essentials; to trust that what is needed will be given there where I am, and to accept and work with what is given—the firmness or softness of the mattress, the food, and the accessibility to a gym or a pool.

The life of a troubadour taught me the simplicity of the gospel, detachment, to trust that what is needed will be given, and gratitude when it is. It also helped me cultivate mindfulness in the present moment and gave me a graceful window into how the Holy Spirit is working in individual lives, in local churches, and in people of other faiths. It has not always been easy or comfortable, but it has been rich and blessed. I remain grateful for all of the enriching experiences along the way.

NOTES

CHAPTER 3

1. *Fasting Rediscovered: A Guide to Health and Wholeness for Your Body-Spirit* (New York: Paulist Press, 1981); *The Sacred Art of Fasting: Beginning to Practice* (Nashville, TN: SkyLight Paths, 2005).

CHAPTER 15

1. Thomas Reese, *National Catholic Reporter*, August 20, 2019.

CHAPTER 17

1. Silvano Giordano, ed., *God Speaks in the Night: The Life, Times, and Teaching of St. John of the Cross* (Washington, DC: ICS Publications, 1991, 2000).

CHAPTER 18

1. For more on this, see my book *Praying by Hand, Praying with Beads* (Mahwah, NJ: Paulist Press, 2019).

CHAPTER 19

1. For more on this topic, see my books *Fasting Rediscovered: A Guide to Health* and *Wholeness for Your Body-Spirit* (New York: Paulist Press, 1981); *The Sacred Art of Fasting: Preparing to Practice* (Nashville, TN: SkyLight Paths, 2005).

2. Thomas Ryan, “Fasting: A Fresh Look,” *America* magazine, March 6, 2006.

CHAPTER 24

1. Cardinal Joseph Ratzinger, “Letter to Bishops of the Catholic Church on Some Aspects of Christian Meditation,” in *L'Osservatore Romano* 2, no. 16 (January 1990): 9.

2. See www.christianspracticingyoga.com.

CHAPTER 27

1. *Disciplines for Christian Living: Interfaith Perspectives* (Mahwah, NJ: Paulist Press, 1993).

2. See https://stillcircle.wordpress.com/2011/03/24/community-of-the-transfiguration-the-journey-of-a-new-monatic-community-a-review/.